NOT ANOTHER ANOTHER JUNGLE

NOT ANOTHER JUNGLE

COMPREHENSIVE CARE FOR EXTRAORDINARY HOUSEPLANTS

Tony Le-Britton

Contents

Houseplants and me

Plants have always played a huge part in my life. My earliest and fondest memories are of being in the garden or on our allotment. I was blessed to have spent the majority of my childhood with my grandparents, who were both keen gardeners and who inspired my love for plants and gardening. Before I could stand my nana would prop me up at the utility room bench, securing me to the back of a chair with a belt so I was firmly upright and had my hands free to sow seeds and pot up plants. I was pricking out plants before I could even walk!

My nana grew most things from seed; she filled the garden with flowers all summer long and she had a beautiful collection of houseplants on the windowsill that thrived in the humidity caused by a constant flow of laundry being washed and dried around them. My grandad was a very traditional grower; he loved growing vegetables, all immaculate and in uniform, straight lines – not a weed in sight. He had a broad knowledge that he had gained over many decades from his elders and from years of trial and error.

My first collection of plants was a rockery. Most children my age (then around five) carried their toys around with them, but I had a trike with a trailer on the back that I filled with soil and rocks and planted up with little pieces of campanula, sempervivum, and sedum that I'd pulled out from the cracks in the wall. It was my pride and joy, but I do have very vivid memories of the stench that came from it when it filled with water that would sit there for days. That was my earliest lesson in the importance of drainage!

In my teenage years I moved on from that trailer to collecting orchids, and I dedicated my interest to these plants until I was in my mid-twenties. For my sixteenth birthday I was allowed to pick one special orchid from Burnham Nurseries, in Devon, and I also received another Phalaenopsis to add to my collection (I still have it today, more than sixteen years later). This tiny collection grew to over 100 orchids, which filled my apartment before I had to rehome all but that one Phalaenopsis when I moved to South East Asia. Through living in Asia, and having the opportunity to explore the Galapagos Islands, Borneo, the Amazon, and the Andes, too, my love of tropical plants really took hold.

When I returned to the UK I added some more houseplants to my collection, but it wasn't until I moved into a flat with no garden that I started to collect these rarer plants more extensively and create my own jungle garden indoors. I even sacrificed my spare room to house a walk-in greenhouse so I could grow my tropicals in optimum conditions. In late 2021, my 'hobby' went to another level. I was walking through my local town and spotted a run-down shop building that I thought would make a beautiful plant shop. I wasn't looking to open a business, but then I realized this would allow me to dedicate more of my working day to doing what I love and enable me to use all of the knowledge I had accumulated to propagate and sell plants professionally.

After a long renovation, in 2022 the doors to Not Another Jungle swung wide open and people travelled from all over the UK (and even from around the world) to attend the opening. I propagate many of the plants I sell, and the ethos behind the shop and this book is to arm people with all the information they need to grow on, cultivate, and even propagate their own plants successfully. I want to make sure that enthusiasts choose a plant that is right for their specific growing conditions – my aim is to enable everyone to be successful with houseplants. I also want to inspire them to explore plant growing and to cut

down on unnecessary waste by keeping their plants going longer and rejecting the throwaway plant culture. It's a win-win. The feeling that comes from nurturing individual living things and seeing them grow is something that can't be rivalled. Rare and unusual plants often demand more detailed care than many of those cultivated for the current houseplant market if they are to truly thrive, so for all you fellow houseplant enthusiasts out there, I'm going to be your guide to caring for those plants so they achieve their full potential.

I love this riot of colour, shape, and texture on a repurposed shelving unit in my shop. It looks fantastic and showcases a huge variety of large, small, climbing, and hanging plants.

GETTING STARTED

In this book I'm going to help you to take your houseplant growing to the next level, by sharing my knowledge as both a home and professional grower, explaining how to care for and nurture your plants, but also the reasons behind why we do what we do for them and why plants behave in certain ways.

Indoor habitats

I love the natural world and often combine my love of travel with my passion for plants. Seeing the terrain and environment in which these plants grow in the wild, and absorbing information from the locals who have cultivated these species through generations, has armed me with essential knowledge about how they grow and what they need to thrive. That said, observing plants outside of their usual habitat is also hugely beneficial – whether in unusual outdoor locations, glasshouses, or even homes. Some plants can be documented growing well in a damp spot beneath the jungle canopy, but to see them flourishing in a crack in a rock in full sun on the side of the road or along a cliffside is also fascinating.

I see influences in how I garden from both inside and outside, because growing houseplants, for me, is just gardening. It's an extension of my garden, but one that allows me to grow a wide variety of plants that I couldn't grow outdoors in the UK climate and that I can cultivate all year round, no matter what the weather.

I like to find the best spots for these plants indoors so they feel at home – but not so that they get too comfortable and take over! My current home has allowed me to have plants both inside and outside. Inside, I adapt plants to fit in with my own living environment, giving them the best care but without adding additional humidity that could damage interiors; outside is another matter, though, as they grow in a greenhouse that runs at very high humidity.

The greenhouse

My greenhouse is a little different to most. I built it inside a garage and it faces south so it can take advantage of the sun's light and heat. The temperatures can get very cold here, so I have to minimize heat loss as much as I can in order to limit how much I have to artificially heat the greenhouse. To do this I have insulated the sides and roof of the building to retain heat.

Although the greenhouse is heated year round, I drop the thermostat to 10°C (50°F) during the winter months, which the plants don't seem to mind – they just slow slightly in their growth. They are used to these lower temperatures, because even during summer the evening temperatures can drop to 10–15°C (50–59°F) in the UK.

Having the greenhouse allows me to grow humidity-loving plants such as Begonia outside of terrariums, or glass or plastic boxes, which wouldn't thrive inside my less-humid home. Many of the other plants I grow in the greenhouse could be adapted to growing in my home with no added heat or humidity, but they grow faster and larger in an environment where I can closer mimic their natural habitat.

The greenhouse creates the perfect environment for these plants, and it's my escape back to the tropics too.

↑ My kitchen, with plants in each corner, on the ground, hanging off beams and rising up out of large pots, including from left to right: *Pilea glauca, Pseudorhipsalis ramulosa, Thaumatophyllum*

bipinnatifidum, Aeschynanthus marmoratus, Aglaonema 'Key Lime', *Aglaonema* 'Silver Bay', *Aglaonema* 'Peacock', *Monstera* 'Thai constellation', *Rhipsalis baccifera*, and *Monstera deliciosa*.

Buying and sourcing rare plants is one of my favourite things to do. Sometimes I'll be scrolling through social media and happen upon something that piques my interest, while at other times I will scour the internet for something specific. There is treasure to be found amongst plant listings!

Building your rare plant collection

How you buy is impacted by why you are buying. Perhaps you are building a collection of plants from a specific favourite genus, or you are passionate about orchids in general, or variegated plants? Maybe you want to buy rare plants and experiment with propagating them for your own interest, or to create new plants to share or to sell on in your own business? Or maybe you just enjoy plants and being surrounded by them.

I often buy plants as investments – both to have fun with propagating them and to sell on their offspring – while some are purely for my own personal collection.

Sometimes these two intentions cross over where there's something I really want for my own collection but that I think would be great to propagate and swap or sell too.

Whenever I increase my collection, I try to spend as little as possible, preferring to swap specimens with collectors from all over the world. The internet has allowed an online plant community to form, through which I can usually track down most plants I desire. However, there can be problems with illegal poaching of rare plants from the wild (see page 171), so always do your research and try to source your plants responsibly.

How to buy

Some of the rarer plants are available in specialist garden centres, but most of the ones I buy I access from private collectors or direct from specialist growers. There are a few ways in which you can do this.

Buying in person

This is always the safest option because you can get a good, clear look at the plant. When you have the plant in your hands, always do a thorough check of its overall health and look for any signs of pests and diseases. The first thing I examine are the roots, as these can tell you a lot about the plant's health. Place your hand over the top of the pot and tip it upside down, then give it a slight squeeze or tap to release the rootball. Do this gently and carefully so as not to damage the plant, then inspect the roots for signs of pests, disease, or rot – healthy roots should be white, vigorous, and long; brown, crumbly roots indicate the plant is not healthy. If the roots do not look healthy, no matter how much you love the plant, I'd always suggest walking away and finding another one.

Next, look at the leaves – are there signs of pest or disease damage? Look on the undersides, as this is usually where pests like to hang out. Diseased plants I'd avoid, but I'm happy to deal with most pests at home if it's a plant I really like. A short quarantine for a couple of weeks in a storage box away from other plants and some simple maintenance before mixing it with the rest of the collection is all it takes to be confident that you've identified and treated any problems (see chapter on pests and diseases for more advice on this).

This Alocasia is a good example of a healthy root system. Avoid recently potted plants, which won't have established their rootball in the pot.

↑ Cuttings are a really economical way to trade plants with reputable growers through the post.

Ordering online

The advantage of buying online is that you can get a wider range of specialist plants from anywhere in the world without having to leave the house! The downside of buying this way, however, is that you won't see the plant until it arrives, so you can't examine it yourself and you are buying on trust.

Always source your plant from a trusted seller or from someone recommended by people who have dealt with them in the past. There are a huge amount of online plant scams – it's big business. It's not just about the quality of the plants, where they have come from is also very important, to avoid encouraging the illegal sale of plants poached from the wild and all the environmental damage this is causing (see page 171).

I always ask for lots of pictures of any plant and its roots; if you're buying cuttings, it's a good idea to see the mother plant they were taken from to assess its health. If the plant you're buying has chimeral variegation (see page 145) make sure the mother also has a consistent amount of variegation throughout the stems and foliage.

The rarer plants can be expensive, with some reaching tens or even hundreds of thousands of pounds, but luckily there are also a lot of rare plants at much more manageable prices. If something is out of budget, 'swapping up' is a great way to get hold of what you want without breaking the bank. Another option is to invest in plants that you're confident about propagating, then you can sell these new plants and use the money to buy more! I've done this from the beginning, and it's allowed me to amass a collection I could have never afforded to just go out and buy.

Propagation rooms

Last year I decided I wanted to up my propagation game by experimenting with different techniques, but as I'm a bit of a neat freak I didn't want little pots all over the house, so I concentrated them all into my utility room. Upon writing this I had the realization that I've in fact recreated that same space I used to love being in as a child; it's where I do my laundry, right by the boiler, so it's constantly warm even when the rest of the house is cold. Of course, these are the perfect conditions for propagation – and without added heating costs! In here I can experiment to my heart's content, but once the door is closed all of my mess is left behind. I use clear plastic storage tubs when propagating plants. These simple items have changed how I propagate and enabled me to create the perfect warm, humid environment without affecting my home; so no matter what your space, they are the first thing I'd recommend investing in. You can use the lid to pot on and mix substrates, or take cuttings and it works really well to stand plants on to drain after watering – all without affecting the growing plants in the box below. Whether you have a room or just a tiny space on the floor, having a dedicated space where you tend to your plants makes the process easier and more enjoyable. I like to lock myself away, pop some music on, and immerse myself into my plant care.

→ These shelves with LED grow lights maximize the amount of growing space I have and provide optimal conditions for growth.

Keep it in proportion

My plant passion at times can be borderline obsessional! I love to watch my plants grow and see their fascinating adaptations to environments and care, and I've built up quite a collection. However, since I opened my shop I've been working away from home every day, which has allowed me to step back and look at my collection with fresh eyes. I have recently reduced the kitchen jungle by around 50 per cent, which has enabled me to focus on fewer plants and get their care right, as well as free up more space to grow them even larger.

I've never been about numbers, but it's easy for things to snowball over time, so now I'm back to my ethos of fewer plants but growing them really well and that's what I hope you will take away from this book – a passion for plants and a firm knowledge of how to keep them happy and healthy within your home.

↑ Outside of my kitchen jungle I keep plants to a minimum, with simple but dramatic statements like this *Philodendron warscewiczii aurea*.

→ The gorgeous flowers of *Begonia* x *albopicta* f. *rosea* reflect the warm terracotta pot and trail over my kitchen counter top.

LIGHT

Light is necessary for almost all life on Earth to function, and it is by far the most important element in growing houseplants, too. Get this right and your plants will reward you with lush, healthy foliage and a strong shape and form.

The importance of light

Exposing a plant to the correct amount of light is key to healthy plants – whether from a natural or artificial source. Just like us, plants have their own preferences to the length and intensity of light they require and can suffer if they receive too much or too little.

Many houseplants have been specifically cultivated for their ability to tolerate a wide range of lighting conditions – from the bright sunlight of conservatories and windowsills to the gloom of north-facing rooms. However, we still have to give them what they need to ensure optimal growth. Many rare plants are newer to cultivation and aren't as resilient to myriad home settings and lighting, so tend to have specific lighting requirements. In these cases, it's important to know what these are and try to accommodate them.

Having seen many of the plants I grow in my home in their natural habitat has helped me to understand their needs and how adaptive they can be. Through social media I see a huge cross-section of the same plants in various settings around the world – in different climates and in varying light levels – and one thing good growers have in common is they have given their plants optimum light levels. No matter what fertilizers, watering regime, substrate mix, or wizardry you employ, you can't grow plants to their full potential without sufficient light for them to perform their most vital processes.

→ Early morning direct sun allows these plants to flourish.

Photosynthesis

One of the most fundamental reasons why light is so important for all plants is because of how they use it in photosynthesis. This vital function is not only essential for a plant's survival, but is also key in our battle against climate change (see opposite).

This is undoubtedly a topic that you covered in biology lessons at school. For me, learning about photosynthesis cemented not only my love for plants but my fascination and respect for them, too. Plants can often fade into the background of everyday life as just a pretty adornment in your home or garden, but they have been quietly and efficiently turning the sun's rays into energy they can use to grow for the last 500 million years. From the grass we walk on to the trees that tower above us, all plants are involved in this complex series of reactions that occur during daylight hours, and, of course, this also happens with our houseplants, whether in natural or artificial light.

How it works

Photosynthesis, put simply, is the process of a plant capturing energy from light and using it to convert the carbon dioxide (CO_2) it takes from the air and the water (H_2O) it takes from substrate into oxygen (O_2) and glucose. The plant retains the glucose, which is a form of sugar, as energy to help the plant to grow, and releases the oxygen back into the air as a waste product. The stomata on the plant – microscopic openings over its surface – are crucial in this process as they enable this exchange of gases.

Another important element in this process is chloroplasts. If you go back to your biology lessons again you will remember the chloroplasts within a plant's cells are home to chlorophyll. The role of chlorophyll is to absorb this light energy and store it in molecules – chloroplasts (see opposite) – in the plant for when the plant needs them.

It is chlorophyll that makes plants appear green to us, because they absorb blue- and red-light wavelengths and reflect back green. It might seem to the observer that some plants do not have chlorophyll, because their leaves are not green and are instead colours such as red or silver. This different colour can be permanent or temporary and can even transition to green as the plant matures, but even in these coloured plants, chlorophyll is still present, it's just been masked by another pigment.

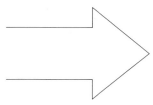

Light
Plants capture energy from light and use it in the process of converting carbon dioxide and water into glucose and oxygen.

Carbon dioxide
Carbon dioxide (CO_2) in the air enters through the stomata (pores) on the plant's surface.

+

Water
Water (H_2O) is taken up by the roots and transported by xylem vessels in the stems to the leaves.

Chlorophyll
Chlorophyll absorbs light energy which is stored by the plant in chloroplasts.

Glucose
A type of sugar that the plant converts light energy into, which it uses to fuel growth.

+

Oxygen
This gas is created as a product of photosynthesis and is released through the stomata into the air.

← The process of photosynthesis.

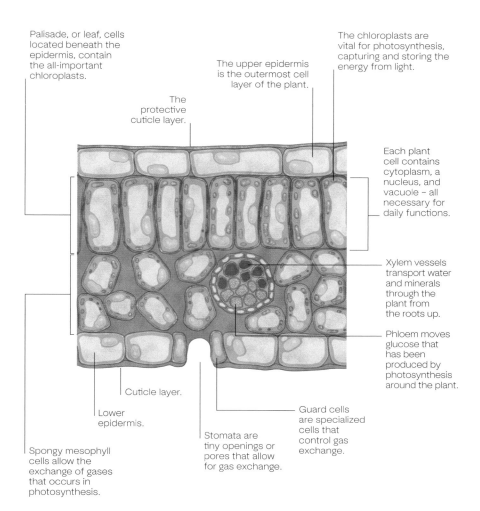

Palisade, or leaf, cells located beneath the epidermis, contain the all-important chloroplasts.

The protective cuticle layer.

The upper epidermis is the outermost cell layer of the plant.

The chloroplasts are vital for photosynthesis, capturing and storing the energy from light.

Each plant cell contains cytoplasm, a nucleus, and vacuole – all necessary for daily functions.

Xylem vessels transport water and minerals through the plant from the roots up.

Phloem moves glucose that has been produced by photosynthesis around the plant.

Cuticle layer.

Lower epidermis.

Stomata are tiny openings or pores that allow for gas exchange.

Guard cells are specialized cells that control gas exchange.

Spongy mesophyll cells allow the exchange of gases that occurs in photosynthesis.

Why is photosynthesis important?

Aside from being a vital process that enables the plant to grow, photosynthesis is also invaluable in the fight against climate change, because plants remove harmful carbon dioxide from the atmosphere. In addition, they have the ability to change atmospheric carbon dioxide into carbon, which is then stored in the plants' leaves, stems, roots, and the soil they inhabit. This is called carbon sequestration, which is being encouraged globally under the Kyoto Protocol. This is an international treaty amongst industrialized nations who have signed up to reduce greenhouse gas emissions, which was agreed in response to the impact of these emissions on climate change.

Plants are also the only living things on the planet that can take energy from the sun's rays and convert it into energy that they can use. This clever adaptation makes them the primary producers in the ecosystem and it also makes them an autotroph – an organism that can produce its own food. The energy they harvest from the sun is transferred into other living things as and when they consume the plant, making them important constituents in the food chain.

Cacti and succulents

While it's true that all plants photosynthesize, not all plants photosynthesize in exactly the same way.

Cacti and succulents are perfectly adapted to their hot, dry climate, having extra water-storing capabilities, but also in the way they photosynthesize. While the stomata of most plants are open during the day to collect carbon dioxide (see page 26), for plants in these arid habitats this would result in huge amounts of water loss through transpiration. So instead these plants have evolved to photosynthesize using CAM (crassulacean acid metabolism).

The basis of this form of photosynthesis is still the same – taking carbon dioxide, water, and energy from the sun and creating sugars and oxygen. But *how* they complete this process is very different. These plants can only photosynthesize during the day when there is available sun, but they also require carbon dioxide at the same time. So because the stomata have to remain closed during the day in order to prevent water loss, they have evolved to store carbon dioxide ready to use when conditions are right. The stomata open at night when the temperatures are lower and the relative humidity is higher (see page 88), and it is then that they capture all the carbon dioxide that they need.

However, because plants cannot photosynthesize at night, they convert the carbon dioxide into malic acid and store it in their cells. They then keep it there until it can be used to complete photosynthesis, when there is available light and the stomata are closed once more.

In the home

Outside, generally you don't need to worry about your plants getting enough light to photosynthesize, as long as you are not planting them into deepest darkest shade. However, light levels in most homes are less than optimal, so you do need to give the position of your plants some consideration.

In my house during the winter my main growing space gets pretty low light levels as the sun dips in the sky, merely skimming past my windows briefly in the morning (that is, if there's not a sky full of cloud). It is at these times that it is really important to optimize the plants' ability to photosynthesize.

Dust, grease, and general dirt build-up on leaves will clog the stomata and cause problems. Any build-up restricts the process of gas exchange in photosynthesis, but also acts as a physical barrier to light hitting the leaf. This would reduce the amount of energy from the sun that is available to the chloroplasts as well as limiting the exchange of gases (see pages 26–27).

So it's important to make cleaning leaves a part of your maintenance routine, either by spraying or showering them with water, or by carefully wiping down larger, more robust leaves (see page 81). Never use oils to clean a plant's leaves – oils (even natural plant oils) can clog stomata and their oily finish can also trap more dust and dirt on the leaf. I do understand why people may reach for oils or other leaf-shine products, because they do make leaves appear glossier and more attractive, but many leaves aren't designed to be shiny. In fact, the gloss reflects light and over time these products can reduce the amount of light your plant can absorb because it bounces off them and is then reflected away, starving the plant of the vital light that it needs.

Morphology is, simply put, the physical form and external structure of plants, which is something that we growers like to manipulate for our own aesthetic pleasure, but for plants this is a vital evolution for their own survival.

Plant morphology

The way a plant looks is not something that has happened by chance; the form you see before you will have evolved over time to make the plant the most efficient energy machine possible. The ultimate aim of these adaptations is so that the plant can try to outcompete other living things in its natural habitat for optimum growing space, but also, crucially, to give itself the best chance of reproducing. After all, that's what all living things are designed to do.

Even our cultivated plants retain many of nature's design features that allow them to capture light most effectively, and it is a key consideration of any grower to maintain these important adaptations as they develop new forms.

Leaves and light

To focus on the leaves of houseplants, their size, shape, colour, texture, and reflectiveness can all play a part in how, and how well, a plant can harvest light. As a result, foliage has evolved in part due to the light that their natural habitat provides.

Many of our favourite varieties originate in the lower stories of dense jungle habitats, so these plants have had to adapt to enable maximum absorption of any light piercing through the crowded canopy above. This is why we see very large leaves in this environment that can both overshadow and outcompete leaves below them.

We also see leaves with holes in them, such as plants like Monstera and Rhaphidophora. This adaptation might seem counterintuitive, but in fact these fenestrations (see page 36) aid in light capture by enabling the leaves to spread out over larger areas using the same amount of tissue and not requiring any extra energy to do so.

Another adaptation that can be seen in some plants is corrugation of its leaves – where they appear wrinkled, folded, or ridged (see right). On the *Anthurium veitchii* x pictured, the reason for this unique patterning has not been conclusively found, but on other plants it is thought that this corrugation occurs in order to give the plants greater flexibility in their environment. When plants position their leaves to receive optimal light, it can leave them exposed to damage from elements such as strong wind, but corrugation allows huge leaves to hang freely in the air and bend to avoid excessive damage. I'm often grateful for this adaptation when I accidentally knock my plants in the greenhouse and turn around with my heart sinking to find that they are undamaged!

A. veitchii is a really special plant, and not least for the way its leaves emerge into the world. They unfurl as tiny, fully formed leaves with the corrugation already in place. Even on my large plants the new leaf starts at around 2cm (¾in) in length, but over the coming days and weeks it slowly swells until it reaches up to 1.8m (6ft) long. The young leaves are very soft and pliable, which works in combination with the corrugation so they can hang in the optimum spot for light with minimum risk of wind damage.

Leaves will reach their maximum size depending on the levels of available light, which is why it's important to measure the light in your room and take visual cues from your plants (see page 43). If a plant's leaves aren't increasing in size with each new leaf or reaching the maximum size for that particular plant, it is likely not receiving enough light.

Anthurium veitchii x has a ribbed leaf allowing for greater flexibility and strength.

↑ Plants evolve and adapt over time to their individual environments, which results in myriad colours, shapes, sizes, and textures. These modifications can often help them absorb light more efficiently.

Stems and light

It's not just leaves that are needed for photosynthesis, stems also play a hugely important part, especially in more dense or crowded settings, such as a jungle floor. This is because the stem is able to carry the leaves to a better lighting situation (known as phototropism – see right), whether that is up and towards the light for greater light intensity (positive phototropism) or away from it towards a more shaded, lower-light area (negative phototropism).

Another fascinating plant process linked to a plant's stem is the shade avoidance response. We know that chlorophyll absorbs blue and red light (see page 26), but a plant can actually monitor the levels of red light around it. Since other plants absorb red light too, if the levels reaching a plant are or become low(er) it senses that there are other plants in its vicinity, thanks to their light signals, and the plant can change its body form in response.

In many cases this will mean speeding up its stem growth and reducing leaf size so that it can race to the available light and outcompete its neighbours. This behaviour can result in tall, leggy growth, but once it reaches a more optimal light setting it will return to its normal form and its leaf size will again increase.

Phototropism

This is the orientation of a plant in response to light, which can be seen in plants both 'positively' and 'negatively'. You probably recognize positive phototropism, because we have all witnessed a plant leaning towards the light as it grows, but you might be less likely to have witnessed negative phototropism. The most obvious example can be seen in roots; most roots grow away from light, aided by gravity, but some plants exhibit negative phototropism in another way: their stems deliberately grow towards shadow. Their end goal is to reach the light, but to do this they first head towards shadow, which is likely to be a tree or other vertical surface. Once attached and climbing, the plant heads up towards the light. You can experiment with this easily with your own plants, and it's amazing to watch.

Fenestrations

These beautiful features give us some of the most breathtaking, intricate leaves on the planet.

Plants that possess fenestrations (holes or gaps) in their foliage, such as Monstera, are among some of my favourites. I particularly like the heavily fenestrated leaves of *M. esqueleto*, with its rows of large asymmetrical holes, or *M. obliqua* 'Filamentous', with tiny thread-like filaments holding the leaf together.

I love the challenge of getting a plant to grow larger and more fenestrated leaves, but before we discuss how to do this, it's worth understanding why we think plants have them and how they have come about. There are many different theories as to why certain plants get holes and fenestrations in their leaves. Two leading theories are that a fenestrated leaf can cover a greater surface area, thus increase its chances of capturing light while not increasing the amount of leaf tissue to support. The other is that fenestrated leaves allow wind to pass through larger leaves, reducing any damage caused. There are many more ideas, and I personally believe there is likely one main factor with several contributing factors as to why evolution favoured plants with fenestrated leaves.

So how does it happen? It's a process called programmed cell death (or PCD). It sounds scary but it's used throughout nature (including in the formation of our fingers). Cells that the plant no longer require commit suicide, activated by a death programme. Wherever these cells die, they leave behind beautiful fenestrations and gaps between our fingers.

The million-dollar question is how to encourage fenestrations on your plant. Luckily this is easily achievable – get your plant climbing on a pole as soon as possible and make sure it has enough light. This simple trick replicates a plant's natural instinct to find a tree in the wild and climb towards the light, maturing as it ascends.

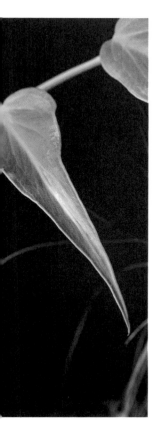

Monstera 'Burle Marx's Flame' showing different stages of fenestration, starting from a young new leaf progressing to a more mature fenestrated leaf (left to right).

NAME *Monstera esqueleto*

FAMILY *Aracaea*

GENUS Monstera

NATIVE RANGE Unknown

HABITAT Unknown

HABIT Climber

TEMPERATURE RANGE 20–30°C (68–86°F)

LIGHT 400–1500 FC

SUBSTRATE Sphagnum moss or chunky aroid mix

HUMIDITY 60%+

WATER Keep moss damp and allow aroid mix to dry by at least 50%

Monstera esqueleto

There is a specimen of *Monstera esqueleto* in Kew Gardens, from where it seems to have moved to other botanic gardens in Europe, but its origins are unknown. It is thought to be a specimen collected from the wild, but as there is no collection data and it has not yet been observed in the wild, it cannot be fully described and registered as a species. 'Esqueleto' means skeleton in Spanish, and this plant is so-called because of the pattern of its fenestrations as it matures, which resemble a rib cage. I've enjoyed growing this plant from a single node into this beautiful specimen – and I've learned a lot, too. The plant pictured is actually the top cutting from my mother plant, and over the last few years I have cut and propagated it many times.

M. esqueleto is a very resilient plant and matures beautifully on a pole. I hope it will enter mass cultivation and we will see it in increasing numbers alongside other iconic plants in its family, such as *Monstera deliciosa* and *Monstera adansonii*. Light is key to producing the huge, deeply fenestrated leaves; it is happy in lower than optimum light, but it will produce smaller leaves and won't reach its potential.

Light is an exact science; while there are varying light levels at which your plants will survive, there are also optimal lighting conditions that will allow your plants to really thrive.

Understanding light

There are some common misconceptions when it comes to houseplant lighting requirements. The first of these is about 'low light'. There is a multitude of plants marketed as low light, but this is only partly true – many do thrive in lower light, but usually when outdoors in their natural habitat. Low light outdoors is brighter and a considerably higher light level than low light in our homes, and there are no plants that will thrive in a very shady corner of a house; some might survive (or die slowly) but none will thrive. You don't need to have optimal light to be able to grow houseplants, but there are some tricks (see page 42) that will help them grow to the best of their ability in a spot with lower light.

Direct and indirect light

There are two types of plants marketed towards low-light spots: either the plants that will survive there, growing very slowly and maybe putting out a new leaf every now and again; or the plants that die slowly, such as the Dracaena, formerly Sansevieria.

This is a great example; Dracaena come from Africa, not shady Africa but hot, dry Africa, and these are recommended as low-light plants because they are really resilient and will degrade very slowly. By the time it does die or start to look ugly, most people will think that it must be something they did, but in actual fact it was just positioned in the wrong light levels all along.

Bright, indirect light is a generalized expression that doesn't really mean anything. If this definition were true, that would mean that almost all houseplants sold with this information written on their label would require exactly the same light levels. Yet obviously this can't be the case, because they all come from such widely different habitats with varying amounts of light. Just because they moved into a two-bedroom semi- doesn't change millions of years of evolution.

To test the claim, I used 50 of my unsuspecting customers as guinea pigs. I asked them to show me where in my shop they thought could be described as bright, indirect light. As you can probably imagine, the results were really varied, but more so than I had anticipated.

I took a measurement using a light meter and the levels ranged from 50 FC (foot-candles, see page 43) to 2500 FC. This is a vast plane of readings, which would have a very varied result in plant growth. A level of 50 FC is too low for all plants indoors and you'd likely see the plant declining fairly quickly, and while 2500 FC would result in very good growth in many houseplants, many plants would need to be gradually acclimatized to these light levels, which could be ultimately too high for others.

This is why understanding what light levels your individual plant really needs and being able to assess the light in your home accurately are so important when choosing plants to bring into your home.

I use a grow light in this dark corner to create optimum conditions where I wouldn't otherwise be able to have plants.

Assessing light

Direct sun is a real luxury to have when growing plants, but all too often houseplants are chauffeured away from direct light in fear it's going to damage them. Of course, too much very direct sunlight can scorch or damage leaves, but a few hours of direct sun in the morning or evening can also be massively beneficial to many houseplants.

If plants are coming straight from a bright atmosphere they will most likely be adapted to that environment, but err on the side of caution when introducing new plants to direct sun. Do it gradually so they can adapt to the higher light levels, at which point they will grow so much more prolifically, achieving faster, larger growth and becoming more resilient to problems like disease. Plants in a higher light spot will also use a lot more water, so remember to monitor them closely as their usual watering may not work in the new spot.

There are four main factors to look at when assessing the lighting in your home ready for your plant purchases:

Light intensity
Consider how strong the light is – is the sunlight direct and shining straight in, or is it diffused by clouds, a window covering, trees, or reflected into the window by a neighbouring building? A minimum of 100 FC (see opposite) is required for most plants' survival but this level should be much higher to grow them optimally. My plants in the house get around 16 hours of light from 500–2500 FC throughout the day for most of the year, but lower levels in winter are still enough to support healthy growth.

Length of light hours
I'd always aim for at least eight hours of light each day. This can be difficult to achieve in some countries or settings, but if you can't reach this length of time, try to up the intensity of the light or subsidize with artificial light if you're noticing your plants exhibiting signs of struggling with the conditions (see page 46).

Colour of your light
If you are growing your plants in natural light this consideration is less important as the colour of the light (see page 26) is already predetermined, but if you're using artificial light it's important to look for a product that has the same Kelvin value as natural light. Anything from 5,000 to 7,000 Kelvin is similar to that of a bright but overcast day and is best for promoting vegetative growth, with 2,000 to 4,000 Kelvin being the better option for promoting flowering and fruiting. The Kelvin value of the lights will be given on the packaging when you buy them, so you can set up your plants with exactly what they need. You can also use these numbers to move particular plants into different locations of natural light to achieve the growth you desire, as Kelvin amounts change throughout the day and depend on weather conditions.

Distance
Of course, it may seem obvious to say, but the distance of a plant from its source of light greatly affects how much light the plant receives. As the distance from the source of light increases its protons are spread over a greater area and so the intensity of that light decreases and covers a greater area – which is called 'inverse proportion'.

The relationship between distance and intensity can be accurately measured using inverse square law, where the light energy is proportional to the square of the distance of the light source from the plant. Light energy remains in proportion to its distance from the source; for example, light energy at twice the distance is spread over four times the area, while light at three times the distance from the source is spread over nine times the area. When you understand this, you can really start to imagine how the light travels and changes through your home and begin to position plants more accurately to provide them with the right light levels.

Measuring light

A light meter is really helpful when you need to identify the light levels in your home. I used to do this by eye, but it's fascinating to see the difference when using actual figures rather than guesswork. I have taken measurements on different days in different weather conditions to give me a broad overview of various growing spots, and I only move plants when the seasons change drastically. I even position plants that like more intense light in front of plants needing lower light levels, to diffuse the light.

Despite having this information, I still experiment and I couldn't recommend it enough – not just with light, but in all aspects of houseplant care. Light is an easy element to experiment with; you can move a plant around and watch how it reacts to the different conditions. Just remember to leave it in one spot for at least a month so you can see the growth from that spot, not a delayed reaction from its previous location.

We can use light to our advantage sometimes, too, even recruiting higher and lower light levels to manipulate a plant into certain behaviours, such as flowering. This is a plant process that can be triggered by a change in light – sometimes an increase in

day length or a decrease as the days get shorter. You can also fake this natural situation by extending the days with artificial lights or darkening the environment for periods to shorten the plants' days.

FC light levels

The FC, or foot candle, is a measurement of light intensity, recording the light reaching a surface rather than the output of the light source, which is why it's relevant in houseplant care. FC is a unit of illumination equal to that given by a source of one candela at a distance of 1 foot; which can be measured using a light meter. FC allows you to measure the light in a particular spot and find the plant that will thrive there. You can also measure the amount of light hitting a plant's leaves to discover how much it is getting and how that affects its growth.

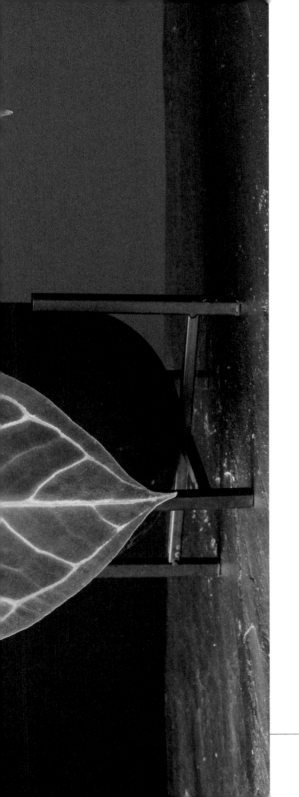

Anthurium magnificum

This beautiful South American plant is a real showstopper. The young leaves almost glow in the light, but resist the temptation to touch them as they are easily damaged. As the leaves grow to their maximum size they begin to darken to almost black, in a clever adaptation to allow the matt leaf to absorb more available light, to cope with living in the shade of a jungle canopy.

The shade *Anthurium magnificum* is used to in the wild is still a lot brighter than the light in most homes. So to achieve huge, distinctive, velvety leaves in a domestic environment, position it in direct light in the early morning or evening to provide enough energy to support growth, but move it away from midday sun, which can bleach or burn the leaves. The large leaves require a lot of nutrition; I add a humus-rich compost into my aroid mix for slow-release nutrition and couple this with fertilizing every other watering. Although its native home is very humid, it will happily adapt to living with no added humidity.

NAME *Anthurium magnificum*

FAMILY Araceae

GENUS Anthurium

NATIVE RANGE Columbia

HABITAT Jungle floor and hillsides

HABIT Terrestial

TEMPERATURE RANGE
15–30°C (59–86°F)

LIGHT 600–1500 FC

SUBSTRATE Chunky aroid mix

HUMIDITY 50–80%

WATER When the pot feels light and mostly dry

Just like every other element of houseplant care, there are some issues that can arise from the light balance in your home being not quite right for your plant. This can easily be corrected with a few simple tricks.

Getting the light right

We know that plants develop adaptations to ensure they receive optimum light levels for growth when in their natural habitats. But while they will also use these in our homes if needed, we do have the opportunity to give them a helping hand to thrive, especially if we don't have houses blessed with a lot of natural light.

So, here are the signs to look out for amongst your plants to detemine if they are struggling with the light levels in your home and need a little intervention.

Too little light

Not providing enough light for your plant can cause stunted, weak, and leggy growth, which can also look pale and insipid. Some telltale signs are plants that lean towards the light, stretching to reach and absorb more than is available in its current spot. Leaves will usually yellow and can even become black and mushy in bad cases.

Another thing to look out for is plants whose substrate stays wet for too long. Overwatering is often attributed to having given the plant too much water, but it can also be a sign of a plant not getting enough light. If a plant is receiving optimal light levels, it's very difficult to overwater it since it will be using water rapidly during photosynthesis and to support new growth. Once you recognize that your plant needs more light, don't move it directly to the brightest spot available. Its leaves are not yet used to strong sunlight, so avoid direct sun initially and gradually increase its light levels. New leaves will emerge, and these will be adapted to this more intense light.

Sometimes aesthetics play more of a part in a plant's location than its health, which means they end up in darker positions than they can cope with. You might have a shady corner or a downstairs loo with very little light but still want a plant there. Many homes are just not designed for plants, but it doesn't mean you can't have them. I get asked about this all the time in the shop, and I always recommend one of two things. The first is an LED grow light on a timer. Cheap and easy to install, this allows you to grow most plants. The other option is to choose a more resilient plant and commit to moving it to a spot with more light twice a week for the whole day. That's not ideal but it will really allow a plant to survive and grow, albeit slower than if it was permanently positioned in optimal light.

Too much light

Getting the balance right is crucial; if the light intensity is too high it can scorch or burn leaves – especially when it causes a high temperature on the leaf's surface. This may not show up immediately, but hours or days later it may present itself as yellowing or completely bleached leaves. Sometimes leaves will brown and crisp, too.

Giving a plant too much time in light can cause many of the same issues. You may see leaves turning away from the light, or some of the other signs mentioned above.

Intense light or a long length of time in light will also cause substrate to dry out rapidly, so when the days begin to lengthen or the weather warms up, be sure to keep a closer eye on your substrate and manage your watering accordingly.

SUBSTRATES
& POTTING UP

Giving your plants the best opportunity to thrive and look their best starts from the soil up. Ensuring the mix is just right means you're providing your plants with all the necessary nutrients to keep them happy and healthy.

The role of substrates

When purchasing your plant it will most likely come already potted, but if you are potting up cuttings or seedlings, or repotting plants, it is important to get the growing media, or substrate, right.

Knowing how and where a plant grows in the wild can help to inform how and where you grow it in your home (see more on this on page 52). But unlike plants that grow outside, the roots of indoor plants are bound within the confines of their pot, so we have to create the perfect conditions for them to thrive – and that starts with the right substrate. This is why my focus in growing indoor plants is always on soil health, because this in turn promotes a robust root system that can support a healthy plant.

To create the optimum environment for pots, each plant requires its own tailored substrate mix that will reflect both its natural habitat and the conditions within your home. The substrate mix that you use can also be dependent on your own personal preference for materials and their availability, as well as their suitability for particular species. The ideal substrate should do three things: physically stabilize and anchor your plant, enable the roots to access water, and supply nutrients.

Stabilize your plant

In their natural habitat plants have all sorts of things to deal with, so being stable in their growing space is key to their long-term success. From wind and rain, to interest from animals and even other plants trying to fight for growing space, life in the wild is tough, but the right substrate encourages a healthy root system that will anchor the plants so they are able to produce and support larger leaves and flowers. In our home setting, although our plants are protected from many of these hazards, we can still utilize this tactic to keep our plants upright, to encourage beautiful growth, and to keep them looking their best.

Access to water

Each plant will have on its own, different water requirements, and this can vary wildly from species to species. Substrate plays a big role in managing this, too – some substrates trap water, others will allow excess water to pass through, while some do a little bit of both to achieve the perfect moisture level.

The substrate ingredients listed on pages 54–57 all have different characteristics, and these can be combined to create a mix that's suitable for a specific plant's needs or your own personal preferences.

Supply nutrients

Substrates can also help to feed our plants in several ways. Organic substrates such as compost or bark decompose and release macro- and micronutrients (see page 54), and are also home to beneficial microbes that can convert and hold on to these substances in the soil. Substrates can also be useful for storing applied nutrients such as fertilizers (see page 98). Adding a topdressing will not only allow the soil to hold on to water but also any fertilizer within it. Then as the plant absorbs the water it can also access all the sustenance contained within the substrate.

The roots are the lifeline for all plants, giving support, and accessing food and water.

Recreating their natural habitat

While many plants will grow in a generic houseplant mix, they will never fulfil the same potential that they would if they were given a substrate tailored to their needs. Imagine if we were all forced to live in the same houses and without an environment around us that helps us as individuals to thrive? Most of us would be unhappy and never reach our full potential, and our plants are no different.

To find the right substrate it's worth looking at how and where our plants would grow in their natural habitats, as this will tell us exactly which ingredients we should use in our mix to create a home away from home where they will flourish. I always start with the basics: does it grow on the ground (terrestrial) or on another plant (epiphyte)? From here we can start to narrow down our options and, using the ingredients on pages 54–57, create a beautiful mix that is curated for each plant.

Don't forget that where you are going to grow the plant will also affect how you compose your mix. For example, the mix you create for a Monstera in your home may be different to a mix you'd use for the same plant in a terrarium or greenhouse. This is because the growing conditions are vastly different – a free-draining mix used in your home might dry out quicker than one in a more humid position, so in this situation it is better to use a mix that is more moisture-retentive. (See page 58 for more advice on creating a really good base mix and how to adjust it.)

← *Philodendron verrucosum* growing up a tree in the Amazon basin before rooting down.

← *Anthurium corrugatum*, a terrestrial plant growing in Ecuador.
→ Mosses and ferns cover every surface in the highlands of

Types of substrates

Here is a selection of commonly used substrates (see pages 56–57 for easy identification), which are widely available through garden centres and online. You can use these in combination to get the perfect mix for your plant's needs (see page 58 for my own favourite mix).

1. Compost

Commonly used, compost is a broad term that describes a soil-like material. It can be made from many different ingredients, but its base usually consists of decomposed organic matter. Peat was traditionally used as compost for many decades, however, the importance of peat bogs' ability to store carbon and reduce carbon emissions has now been recognized. As a result, there is a global call for products containing peat to be removed from sale, and while this campaign continues, many incredible alternatives are being created. Peat-free composts are made from a wide range of organic materials, including bark, composted wood fibre, coir, and even sheep's wool, and many are focused on being environmentally friendly. I include highly nutritious living compost – one that contains beneficial microbes and is not sterilized – as a base in almost all my mixes.

2. Bark and coco chips

These are fantastic substances to use as a growing material for orchids and some other epiphytic (air-growing) plants, or as part of a mix for other plants. They offer moisture retention while allowing water to pass through without pooling at the roots. Bark chips are available from various trees and coco chips are made from the shell of coconuts. Both can be used fresh or partially composted and are long-lasting, decomposing slowly. Note that as bark decomposes it removes nitrogen from the soil so it's important to add fertilizer to this substrate.

3. Akadama

Akadama, meaning red ball clay in Japanese, is used throughout Japan and worldwide by bonsai growers. I recently discovered it on a trip to a specialist Begonia grower in the Netherlands. Since then I've trialled it in my own Begonia collection and it works tremendously well. Akadama are small dried clay balls available in different sizes. They are fantastically water- and nutrient-retentive, while their structure allows water and all-important oxygen to move through the substrate freely, preventing root rot. This is particularly beneficial with Begonia, as these plants can rot easily because of their high-humidity environment.

4. Vermiculite

Vermiculite is more moisture-retentive than perlite (see below) although it offers less aeration. It wicks away and stores water, making it available to plants as and when they need it and helping to keep an even moisture throughout the mix. Vermiculite does not deteriorate.

5. Perlite

This is a naturally occurring mineral that is heat-treated to high temperatures. When heated it multiplies in size but not weight, making it incredibly light. It's a really useful material because it adds volume and air to a compost mix, but it also holds on to water on its outside surface, which leaves it available to roots. However, I don't find this substrate visually appealing, and it does tend to float to the top of a pot when the plant is watered.

6. Sand

Horticultural sand can be found in many pre-mixed compost mixes, and adding extra can also be beneficial in improving drainage, especially for plants from areas of drought, such as succulents, that don't like their substrate to be too wet.

7. Grit

I've started to use a little horticultural grit in some of my mixes, especially those for plants in very humid conditions, such as my propagation boxes. Added to any mix, this grit will open up the soil structure, allowing more air flow and improving the water drainage. This is a fantastic addition to compost for drought-loving plants, or can be used as a topdressing to help prevent water loss through evaporation.

8. Sphagnum moss

Sphagnum moss is one of my favourite substrates to grow in because of its versatility. It is important to conserve this natural material, so never collect it from the wild, instead buy it live or dried. Both have fantastic water-storing capabilities and can be used either on their own or as part of a mix. I use live sphagnum moss, which is harvested sustainably and under licence, which I then grow on at home and use as and when I need it. I find it fantastic for rooting cuttings in as well as for growing adult plants.

9. Activated charcoal

I don't use charcoal, as I see no benefit to my plants' health when I do, but it is believed to rid soil of impurities, hold on to nutrients and provide aeration. For these reasons, it's particularly popular with terrarium growers and as part of contained, living ecosystems.

10. Cork bark

Cork bark is not only beautiful to look at but fantastic for mounting epiphytic plants onto. Its rough texture allows plant roots to fuse to it, and it also holds on to moisture well.

11. Pon

Pon is a soil-free plant substrate. It's a purely mineral plant substrate and is usually used with a water reservoir at the base of the pot. It has gained popularity in recent years, although I'm personally not a fan because I find the living environment provided by a soil- or moss-based substrate is better for plant growth.

12. LECA

LECA, or Lightweight, Expanded Clay Aggregate, is another soil-free growing media. Used alone it is usually put into a self-watering pot or one with a reservoir where the clay balls can wick up excess water around the plant's roots, preventing them becoming waterlogged, and enabling them to absorb water as and when they need it. I don't grow in LECA but it can be a great addition to a soil mix to retain moisture and aerate it.

Coir/coco peat

Coir opens up and lightens the structure of a compost mix and has great water-holding capabilities, although indoors I do find it becomes hydrophobic (water-repellent) if it's allowed to dry out past a certain point. Many commercial growers have moved away from peat and now use coir, or coco peat, as an alternative, although its eco credentials are currently unclear and in dispute. To avoid this issue, I've managed to remove coir from my houseplant mix by using 20 per cent partially composted bracken instead (see page 58).

1 Compost

2 Bark and coco chips

5 Perlite

6 Sand

9 Activated charcoal

10 Cork bark

3 Akadama

4 Vermiculite

7 Grit

8 Sphagnum moss

11 Pon

12 LECA

My mix

I'll let you into a little secret. I make up one large barrow of mix, which with a little bit of jiggery pokery I can use for most of my plants. It is a combination of 20 per cent unpasteurized compost that is made from composted sheep's wool and bracken, along with 20 per cent partially composted bracken, and the final 60 per cent is a 50/50 mix of small and large bark chips. It makes a fantastic base that I can tweak for each plant for their specific requirements.

If you're repotting a plant that requires a more free-draining combination, shake your box of pre-made mix and the larger ingredients will rise to the top, giving you a chunkier substrate. If something requires a more moisture-retentive, finer mix, the substrate that's sunk to the bottom will be perfect. Keeping this mix prepped and to hand in a sealed box is not only convenient, but it also ensures it maintains an even moisture and allows beneficial microbes to develop, so it's ready to support your plant whenever you need it.

TIP If your plant isn't ready for a full repot, scrape away 2.5cm (1in) or so of the substrate from the surface and replace it with fresh. This is a great way to quickly boost your plants with a hit of nutrients.

REPOTTING PLANTS

If you have noticed a reduction in leaf size or speed of growth of your plant, it could be time for a repot. Repotting creates more space for the plant to grow a larger root system, and also adds more available, much-needed nutrients into the pot with some fresh substrate. It's important to only repot into a container one or two sizes larger, as placing a plant into a pot that is too big can easily lead to under- or overwatering.

You will need Substrate mix | Larger plant pot | Water

1. Prepare the substrate mix for your plant and add a layer to the base of the new pot to just cover it, allowing plenty of space for the plant's rootball.

2. Place one hand over the top of the planted pot and turn it upside down. A gentle squeeze or tap on the sides of the pot should release the rootball.

3. You can now put the plant into the new pot, making sure to position it at the same depth as it was in the original pot.

4. Fill around the rootball with the new substrate, and firm down. Tapping the sides or the base of the pot will help your substrate to settle.

5. Water your plant well. Let the water soak through the pot, shake to remove any excess, then allow to drain thoroughly before returning to its position.

NAME *Monstera obliqua*
'Peruvian form'

FAMILY Aracaea

GENUS Monstera

NATIVE RANGE Peru,
South America

HABITAT Jungle

HABIT Low-level climber

TEMPERATURE RANGE 20–30°C
(68–86°F)

LIGHT 100–400 FC

SUBSTRATE Sphagnum moss
or chunky aroid mix

HUMIDITY 70%+

WATER Keep evenly moist

Monstera obliqua
'Peruvian form'

The complex (a group of closely related organisms) of *Monstera obliqua* contains many different plants rather than one species. Some clones of *M. obliqua* have fenestrations and others do not, but *M. obliqua* 'Peruvian form' falls in the former camp and is by far the most famous and most spectacular clone. Its highly perforated leaves are miraculous, with some parts held together only with thread-like filaments.

This variety is small compared to most of the other *Monstera* in the genus, making it a wonderful plant to grow at home. I grow this plant in living sphagnum, which I keep evenly moist at all times, although it can be grown successfully in a chunky aroid mix. For optimal growth I keep humidity above 70 per cent by growing it in a cloche, with a daytime temperature of 30°C (86°F) dropping to 20°C (68°F) overnight. Its lighting requirements are somewhat lower than those of other *Monstera*, as it naturally grows lower down in the jungle, and I've found an optimum level of 100–400 FC works well at home.

The right pot not only changes the way a plant looks but also how it grows. However, to achieve a healthy, happy and good-looking plant, you also need to support it, especially when growing climbers.

Choosing the right pot or pole

I have fairly simple taste when it comes to pots, because I love the plant itself to be centre stage of any display. That said, getting the right shape, height, and material definitely matters when choosing a pot, in order to ensure the best growing conditions for your plant.

Some plants – in particular climbers – also require a little vertical support as they grow. If this is the case, allowing enough space to partially bury a pole alongside the plant is a key consideration. When selecting a pot, make sure it is wide enough to accommodate both.

Terracotta
An unglazed terracotta pot is my all-time favourite. Terracotta is porous so it allows air to move in and out of the pot and allows water to evaporate. It's perfect for use in high humidity or wet environments like terrariums, cabinets, or greenhouses and decreases the risk of overwatering greatly. This also makes it a great option in the home for any chronic overwaterers or for drought-loving plants. I plant direct into it, just make sure there is a drainage hole in the bottom, and you put a drip tray beneath it to catch any excess water.

Display pots
The majority of the plants around my home are housed in plastic nursery pots, which

I then drop into display pots. This makes for easy watering, as any excess liquid is caught in the pot below. If you are worried about overwatering, take the plant out of the display pot to water it and place it back in once it has drained. I prefer my plants not to be overshadowed by a pot, so I usually use plain black pots. These also warm up in the sun and hold residual heat, which can promote better root growth – a fantastic tip for growing cuttings!

Hanging plants

Some of my favourite plants are growing in hanging pots, and I find this works really well for trailing and epiphytic ('air-growing') plants. Hanging plants up means you get to view them at eye height, which is often their best angle, not to mention the fact that this adds another dimension to your home by using vertical spaces. These pots also allow you to grow much larger plants without taking up floorspace, and you can pop them in the best-lit spots around the house.

Plant supports

When putting climbing plants into pots, for best results they should be given a pole as early as possible to support their growth. Giving them a surface to climb on mimics their natural habitat and will result in a more vigorous plant and larger leaves, and it also encourages them to reach maturity and flower. Initially the plant needs to be tied to the pole to encourage it to climb, but it will quickly learn to attach itself. I'm often asked how to cultivate or increase fenestrations and my answer is always: give your plant a pole and let it climb (see Light, page 36).

Poles come in myriad materials, with commercial ones made of coir – plants can grip to these as they grow, but this material in particular doesn't hold moisture well. This is a disadvantage, as materials that hold moisture will allow roots to penetrate it and extract more water and nutrients, which will support faster, larger growth. Popular, effective pole materials include moss, felt, and natural bark.

Black pots contrast with the foliage and allow the plants to take centre stage.

↑ Terracotta is a great pot material for people who overwater or in higher humidity enviroments. Plants from left to right: *Pilea glauca*, Sarracenia, *Epipremnum pinnatum* 'Marble', *Aglaonema pictum* 'Tricolor', *Alocasia micholitziana* 'Variegata'.

↑ The right pot or pole allows the plant to be displayed at its best. From left to right: *Begonia darthvaderiana* x *malachosticta, Tradescantia zebrina, Alocasia melo, Rhaphidophora tetrasperma* 'Variegata'.

NAME *Epipremnum pinnatum 'Cebu blue'*

FAMILY Aracaea

GENUS Epipremnum

NATIVE RANGE Cebu Island, Phillipines

HABITAT Mountainous tropical forest

HABIT Climber

TEMPERATURE RANGE 15–34°C (59–93°F)

LIGHT 500–1500 FC

SUBSTRATE Live sphagnum moss or aroid mix

HUMIDITY 50–80%

WATER Damp

Epipremnum pinnatum 'Cebu blue'

This rare and beautiful plant is one of very few aroids with this unique matt, steely blue foliage, and this makes it much in demand amongst collectors. When immature the plant has solid, lance-shaped leaves, with a more intense colour. As it matures, though, it develops tiny holes and deep-cut fenestrations and the colour becomes greener while retaining a steely blue shift.

It's a resilient plant that will grow in a multitude of conditions, but to reach maturity it must be allowed to climb and have access to light. A bright spot with several hours of direct sun each day is optimal. In a regular home environment, allow the substrate to dry out by at least 50 per cent before watering, but in a high-heat/humidity environment it can be kept damp. I apply a liquid fertilizer in every other watering to support the most rapid growth and allow the plant to reach its full genetic potential.

HOW TO MAKE A MOSS POLE

This is how I make my moss poles to support my climbing plants. The advantage of making your own is that these can be easily extended by adding on another section if the plant outgrows them.

You will need Substrate | Pot | Black or dark green mesh | Pliers | Damp moss | Cable ties
Climbing plant | Metal pins

1. Put a little substrate into the base of the new pot as if you were repotting (see page 59). Cut the mesh to size for your pole – always make the pole taller than your plant to allow for growth.

2. Place the half-rolled mesh on a flat surface, fill down the middle with damp moss, leaving a gap at the base that is the same depth as your pot. This section will be buried in the substrate.

3. Roll the mesh around the moss to make a long 'pole'. Secure tightly using cable ties. Once secure, fill gaps by pushing in moss from the open tube top.

4. Secure the plant to the moss pole using metal pins so the roots are just below the base of the moss.

5. Fill the empty base of the pole with the same substrate you are using in your pot and place it into the pot with the plant.

6. Fill around the pole and plant with substrate.

Thigmomorphogenesis

I witnessed this fascinating process in action in my home with my own collection of orchids.

I had so many plants that I placed wires around a room to hang the pots from. Some hung in doorways, which meant I bumped into these as I walked past. These plants grew visibly larger and more prolific root systems, and on noticing this, I tested this by swinging every other orchid on the line a couple of times per day. Again, these grew more roots. I concluded it was a reaction of the plant to the wind or movement that enabled it to secure itself more safely.

Then a couple of years ago, while on a visit to the Eden Project in Cornwall, I asked one of the gardening team about the depth of their tree roots and how many of their large trees fall inside the biospheres. They told me that they open the windows regularly to allow the wind through, because this movement stimulates the trees to produce more roots and stabilize themselves. They went on to explain 'thigmomorphogenesis' to me, which was a term I'd not heard before – a plant's response to mechanical sensation. This could be anything from the impact of wind and rain to insects and passing animals, and this causes changes to a plant's morphology (see page 30). You've seen the videos of the person shaking the fiddle leaf fig, well, they are doing this because it stimulates the plant to produce more roots and also a shorter, stronger stem.

My happy hanging orchids, left to right: *Tolumnia*
'Jairak Rainbow', *Dendrobium unicum*,
Mediocalcar umboiense, Dendrobium sulcatum.

NAME *Masdevallia coccinea*

FAMILY Orchidacea

GENUS Masdevallia

NATIVE RANGE Colombia

HABITAT Cloud forest

HABIT Terrestrial

TEMPERATURE RANGE
8–21°C (46–70°F)

LIGHT 800–1500 FC

SUBSTRATE Sphagnum moss
or orchid bark

HUMIDITY 60% +

WATER Substrate should remain damp

Masdevallia coccinea

A cool-growing orchid from the cloud forest of Colombia, *Masdevallia coccinea* has a long flowering period with blooms of a dazzling, almost luminous colour and deep velvety finish. Its native forests are cool, humid, and have good airflow, so replicating this at home will promote blooming – which is most often between March and August but this can happen throughout the year. Use a slightly taller pot for this species as it has long roots and will naturally push itself out of the substrate if the pot is too shallow. I prefer unglazed terracotta to allow air circulation through the substrate and around the roots. My preferred substrate is sphagnum moss, as it remains damp but allows good drainage, especially when teamed with terracotta. Another option is a fine orchid bark, but this needs replacing as it decomposes to avoid any areas becoming compacted and waterlogged. Avoid direct sun on its leaves – I grow this on the bottom shelf of the greenhouse so it is shaded from overhead artificial lighting but still receives a diffused natural light through the semi-opaque windows.

WATER & HUMIDITY

All plants are reliant on water to grow and have adapted to myriad environments in the wild to seek it out. However, plants in our homes have more restricted access to water by natural means; so this is where we come in.

Watering

Water is essential for all life on Earth, and our own human need for it in order to survive binds us to our plants and reminds us that all living things are not too dissimilar.

While plants growing in the wild have evolved to maximize their water uptake and storage, plants in our homes are entirely reliant on us for water. And of course, this isn't just about getting hold of the water that they need, it's about getting the amount just right, including ensuring there is sufficient drainage to prevent roots becoming waterlogged and then rotting as a result.

When growing plants indoors or even outdoors in pots, there are several factors that are important for ensuring the correct balance of water for the plant, including using the right container (see page 62), filling it with the best substrate designed for specific plants (see page 54), and controlling the light and temperature levels around the plant.

Water is stored in the cell vacuole. With insufficient water the vacuole shrinks and becomes flaccid; as water enters, it enlarges and becomes turgid.

Flaccid cell

Turgid cell

→ Water is a vital requirement of cells to keep a plant physically supported; without it stems and leaves will droop and flop.

Why is water so important?

Water comprises up to 95 per cent of a plant's tissue and is drawn up into the plant from the ground through its roots, travelling up into the stems and then into the leaves through the xylem vessels, which are a bit like the capillaries in the human body. The water carries essential nutrients from the soil into the plant, and the xylem vessels move this nutritious cocktail around the plant, where it can be used to aid its growth and keep it healthy.

Water is also needed by the plant to perform other vital processes. For example, plants couldn't photosynthesize without water. During photosynthesis a plant takes carbon dioxide from the air and hydrogen from the water that is absorbed by the roots and it releases oxygen as a by-product (see page 26).

Water is also responsible for keeping plants supported; the fluid in the cells keeps them turgid, allowing a plant to stand upright whilst also enabling it to bend in the wind or to grow towards the light without breaking.

You will notice how soft and limp plants become when you forget to water them. Sometimes I'll deliberately underwater a plant to make it easier for me to manipulate its stems onto a frame or pole. That sounds mean, but in fact this is kinder to the plant as it is far more flexible in this state and less likely to break. You can then just water it once it is secured in place, ready to grow as you want it to.

How much water is enough?

Different plants have different watering requirements, so always research what each plant needs but do remember that the way in which it grows in the wild may not translate into home growing. For example, many Alocasia grow in very wet or damp conditions in their native habitat, but there they also have high light levels and more intense heat. Since in most homes the light and heat levels are considerably lower than in some outdoor climates, in these situations we must reduce the volume of water given to a plant, too, to protect them against rot.

Once you have your plant in the right spot for its individual light requirements, the only part you need to get right is its watering, and this is one of those things you can only do by getting to know their cues over time. Despite a lot of advice suggesting you should water once a week, plants do not grow on a schedule, so a watering timetable isn't the best approach. I always advise that you check your plants once a week as a general rule, but don't necessarily water them then – do it only when they need watering. I keep my plants around the house and in the shop very dry. It surprises a lot of people but it helps avoid so many problems and allows maximum air circulation to the roots, too.

When to water

There are several telltale signs that your plant may be in need of water, and some easy and foolproof ways to check.

If your plant's leaves look less vibrant and begin to dull, this is often a sign of dehydration. When there is less water in each cell, the leaves may also become more flaccid or start to wrinkle. Ideally, don't allow plants to get to this stage, but if they do, they should recover well after a thorough watering.

Always check your plant needs water before watering. The best way to do this is to learn to sense the weight of your pots. A pot containing moisture feels much heavier than a dry one and the sound of it being placed on a surface is completely different, too – it makes a duller noise. Try picking up smaller containers regularly and learning the

difference; do the same with hanging plants, removing them from their hooks to check. In the long run it will save you so much time and you'll feel confident about knowing when to water.

There is, of course, the simple finger and soil method, too, which is helpful for heavier pots that you can't lift. Press your finger deep into the soil and if it still feels damp, it doesn't need water. Never just press the soil surface to see how wet it is, as this will not give an accurate reflection.

When watering houseplants, the time of day doesn't really matter. However, if you are likely to get the leaves wet, a morning watering minimizes water sitting on the leaves too long and creating an ideal spot for fungus to take hold, as it will evaporate during the day. This is a good rule if you are growing around your home where temperatures, light levels, and airflow are lower, and it is something I do myself. In stark contrast, the plants in my greenhouse are hosed down several times a day because of the high temperature, light, and constant airflow, which helps avoid many issues.

The water I use

I live in an area with very hard water, but I use tap water for all of my plants (except carnivorous plants). My plants grow consistently well with this and I've never had any issues. I'm sure I could improve my plants' growth by looking at other water options, such as distilled water or that produced by the purification process of reverse osmosis, but for the huge cost and effort that would be involved for the latter, I don't think it would be worth it.

How to water

Do you water from the top or the bottom? It's the age-old discussion. Of course, if one method works for you over another, stick with it, but there are some definite pros and cons you should consider before deciding.

I'm a top-waterer – always top, unless I've forgotten to water something for a while and the soil has then become so dry it turns hydrophobic (repels water), in which case I'll bottom-water until the soil is fully hydrated.

I prefer watering from above because it allows me full control; I know exactly how much water is going in. Top-watering also has gravity to its advantage, pulling the water down through the pot, allowing it to flush out any build-up of gases or excess salts from previous watering, or fertilizer that could accumulate and cause root rot or burn (see page 109).

Bottom-watering is much favoured, especially by those with larger collections, because it means many plants can be watered at once together in a large container or bath. The plants should be left for a few minutes so that the soil can absorb as much water as possible before it reaches saturation point.

One amazing sight I've witnessed is when commercial growers in the Netherlands water their plants. Plants on the floor are usually bottom-watered with a flooding system. Through this process, sides raise around each section of plants, then vents in the floor open up to allow water to rush in. The 'containers' fill to several inches deep and the water sits for a while until all plants are saturated. Once complete, the drains open up and excess water ebbs away. It's simple but highly effective – like most of the best inventions.

Personally, I find that bottom-watering oversaturates the lower soil and it only works well in a commercial greenhouse because they have high light and heat levels to prevent the substrate sitting cold and wet for too long, which is the ultimate recipe for root rot.

To help prevent root rot, allow water to drain right through the substrate before returning the pot to its growing position.

NAME Sarracenia

FAMILY Sarraceniaceae

GENUS Sarracenia

NATIVE RANGE North and South America

HABITAT Bogs and wetland

HABIT Ground dwelling

TEMPERATURE RANGE 15–30°C (59–86°F)

LIGHT 1500–2500 FC

HUMIDITY 50%+

SUBSTRATE Low-nutrient, acidic, moisture-retentive mix

WATER Wet

Sarracenia

Found in the nutrient-poor bogs of North and South America, because of this lack of available nutrients in the soil Sarracenia have evolved pitcher-shaped foliage to capture insects and even small amphibians as food. Their bog habitat in the wild means that in the home they must remain wet at all times and be positioned in a bright spot in full sun indoors or outside. Move them somewhere cool but in full sun for around four months over autumn and winter; the drop in temperature and the shorter days will trigger dormancy. You must only use rainwater for these plants, as the salts and chemicals in tap water damage and can kill them.

These plants don't require fertilizer because they get all the nutrients they need from their airborne prey. Insects are lured in by the intricate pitcher design and the plants also secrete a fructose liquid that is irresistible to many bugs. The pitcher is slippery and has downward-pointing hairs, so once the prey enters, it cannot escape and it then decomposes in the liquid at the base of the pitcher.

Spraying

Spraying plants with water can be really beneficial for them, but how much so depends on what you're trying to achieve. In a home environment, spraying will not change the humidity of the room for any sufficient period of time to positively impact your plants. In an enclosed environment like a terrarium or greenhouse, however, spraying to increase humidity does work really well.

What spraying is great for is cleaning away dust and dirt from leaves. Dust, dirt, and pollution build up on leaves, and without regular rain to remove this it will start to affect how efficiently a plant can function. Any build-up decreases the amount of light the leaf and plant can absorb, and the one thing most homes don't have enough of is light, so it is important to maximize this. A spray down in the shower or outside every couple of weeks with a hose will leave your plants looking and feeling great.

Another benefit of spraying is controlling pests; it dislodges pests (see page 159) and also prevents a dry environment, which is something that spider mites thrive in.

When you spray, try to avoid getting too much water into the pot and substrate if the plant itself doesn't need watering. Placing the pot in a bag and tying it closed around the base of the plant to cover the substrate surface works well. Once this is done, spray thoroughly – and don't forget the underside of the leaves – then when you're finished take a microfibre cloth and wipe down the leaves to remove any leftover dirt or pests.

I'd always recommend avoiding applying anything but water to your plant's leaves. Don't be tempted to use detergents or oils to clean leaves or add shine. Detergents can strip the natural oils from the leaves, but applying oils to them can clog the stomata and prevent them doing their job, as well as make dust build up faster (see page 29).

This Dieffenbachia is extremely underwatered but can be saved by cutting back to where the stems are green and fleshy. Then water it well from the base and place somewhere warm and bright and let it recover.

Underwatering

You are far less likely to cause significant damage to a plant by underwatering it than overwatering, and although I do recommend allowing most plants to dry out by at least 50 per cent before watering, prolonged underwatering can damage a plant.

Symptoms

Identifying underwatering is fairly easy. The soil will be very dry and may be shrinking away from the sides of the pot. Slight underwatering will make the leaves appear flaccid and the leaves and stems may wrinkle. Severe underwatering causes crispy browning of leaves or whole sections of the plant.

Plant rescue

In most cases a good drink will quickly rehydrate a plant, but if it has been left too dry for too long you may need to be more active in its rehab. Remedying underwatering is a simple process that causes minimal disturbance to your plant.

When you water, if you're finding that the substrate doesn't absorb or even repels the water being added, this is an indicator that it has become hydrophobic and it will be more difficult to re-wet. The best fix for this is to water your plant as normal and then water it again just 30 minutes later. Alternatively, you can place the pot in a dish of water and allow the growing medium to slowly hydrate from the base upwards.

It's always best to try to avoid the substrate drying out to this point, though, because this level of dehydration will also destroy the microbiology and texture of the growing medium. Adding a layer of fresh compost on the surface of the rehydrated substrate will help improve this and is well worth doing. In severe cases, cut the plant back and water from the base (see on the opposite page).

Overwatering

Overwatering is often cited as the biggest killer of houseplants. This is true to a degree, although the reason why most plants become saturated is because they aren't receiving the optimum amount of light and so they photosynthesize slower, using less water.

In fact, it's very difficult to overwater a plant that receives the right amount of light and is able to function properly and healthily.

Symptoms

There are many things that will alert you to a plant being overwatered. For most plants, it's always best to allow the soil to dry out by at least 50 per cent. If the soil is staying wet most of the time, you are probably watering it too much. Exceptions would be bog plants and most carnivorous plants that do like to remain consistently wet.

If your plant is looking unhealthy, I'd always recommend checking the roots as the first port of call. These will tell you a lot about the overall health of your plant. If the roots are kept wet for a prolonged period of time they may start to rot; when this happens the roots appear black, may feel mushy, and can have a very distinctive smell. The leaves will also give clear signs that a plant is being overwatered; if the roots have begun to rot, the foliage will become flaccid or turn black or brown.

Plant rescue

There are several ways to correct and combat future overwatering. If you suspect you have overwatered your plant and the soil is drying out slowly, remove the plastic nursery pot from the display pot, if you are using one, to increase airflow, which will help wick away excess moisture. Also move your plant to a brighter, warmer spot to encourage more photosynthesis (see page 26), which will use more water.

Sometimes you will only notice that you've overwatered your plant when root rot has already occurred, however, your plant is still salvagable (see page 87).

WATER AND HUMIDITY

NAME Lithops

FAMILY Lithops

GENUS Aizoaceae

NATIVE RANGE Southern Africa

HABITAT Desert and arid environments

HABIT Terrestrial

TEMPERATURE RANGE 20–30°C (59–68°F) during summer with a winter minimum of 5°C (41°F)

LIGHT 2500 FC+

SUBSTRATE 80% pumice, sandy grit with 20% organic matter

HUMIDITY <60%

WATER Allow to completely dry

Lithops

If you don't have much time and have a bright, sunny spot these are for you. A fascinating genus with incredible adaptations, in the wild Lithops grow in harsh, arid conditions, so they have evolved two succulent leaves attached to a root for efficient water storage. Each individual colony has colours and patterns that allow them to blend into their setting and avoid being predated upon by herbivores looking for water. These adaptations make plants incredibly hard to find unless they are in flower. To grow at home, a very free-draining substrate with a small amount of compost is key, to avoid rot.

Lithops have a fascinating growth cycle. They are dormant during summer, to conserve water, and in a very bright spot plants may be flat or just under the substrate – the root contracts and pulls the leaves under to prevent them dehydrating in hot weather. During summer, water sparingly until autumn (or when night temperatures drop below 10°C/50°F), then stop watering until spring (or when night temperatures are consistently above 10°C/50°F). In winter leaves may wrinkle but don't water – the plant uses water and nutrients from old leaves now to create new ones; watering would confuse and kill it.

Guttation

Have you ever woken up to find little pools of water below your plants or droplets on the end of leaves? This is guttation.

Guttation, simply put, is how a plant secretes water from within to balance how much it takes in. It can only occur in plants that have a vascular system because it relies on pressure to push water out through the closed stomata (pores).

Water plays a vital role in photosynthesis (see page 26), so plants have evolved highly efficient ways to take it from the soil. Water is transported through the plant via xylem vessels, taking the water absorbed by the roots up the stem, petioles, and leaves.

A plant only uses 5 per cent of the water it absorbs, while 95 per cent is lost through transpiration. The stomata on a plant's surface absorb carbon dioxide to use in photosynthesis, and release water.

This usually happens during the day, then the stomata close at night, although plants in arid conditions keep their stomata closed during the day to avoid excess moisture loss in heat and open them at night. When the stomata close, water pressure builds in the plant, which is when it will guttate, secreting excess water through the leaf tips.

Guttation is usually nothing to be concerned about and you'll likely witness it more after watering. If it persists and seems excessive, check your plant's roots aren't waterlogged, but in most cases it's just a very visual example of a fascinating plant process in action.

RESCUING A PLANT WITH ROOT ROT

Overly wet soil and excessive watering can cause roots to rot. But this doesn't have to mean the end of your plant, you can restore a healthy root system.

You will need Sharp blade or scissors | Small pot | Free-draining substrate mix

1. Carefully remove the plant from its pot and gently start teasing away excess soil from the roots.

2. Rinse off leftover soil so you can assess any damage to the roots clearly.

3. Identify any rotten roots and use a sharp blade or scissors to cut away any rot. Cut 2cm (¾in) above where the rot ends, as it has likely already started spreading further up the root.

4. Prepare a smaller pot and a free-draining mix for the plant. A smaller pot and a more free-draining substrate will prevent any further overwatering.

5. Water well to settle the substrate around the roots. Shake the pot to remove water pockets, then drain. Placing the plant in a higher heat and humidity aids a faster recovery.

WATER AND HUMIDITY

While we shouldn't hand over our homes to our plants and their needs, some plants – particularly those from humid tropical regions – do require a few easy adaptations that will keep both plant and grower happy.

Humidity

Humidity is the amount of water vapour that is present in the air, and that level increases the more water vapour it holds. Warmer air can hold more water vapour than cooler air if there is water available in the environment, which is why humidity is high in the tropics.

Most often humidity is referred to as relative humidity. This is the amount of water vapour that is in the air expressed as a percentage of the maximum amount that the air can hold at saturation point at the same temperature. So, for example, a room that records 60 per cent humidity when its air temperature is 20°C (68°F) will have a lower relative humidity percentage when the room is warmer.

So while knowing the origins of a plant and being able to mimic the humidity levels of where it naturally grows can mean you will see better growing, this is only true if you can also match other factors, such as temperature.

Five plants of interest

Begonia arachnoidea
Begonia baramensis
Piper porphyrophyllum
Begonia pteridiformis
Corybas roseus

Humidity in the home

Don't get bogged down in whether or not you can provide super-high humidity, though, because leaves are designed to keep water in and keep the plants hydrated. I grow the majority of my plants without added humidity, and the only ones that really need high humidity to grow are placed in the greenhouse and in propagation boxes. All of my plants around the house thrive in a regular humidity of around 60 per cent, which is standard in most homes, and this can drop below 40 per cent if fires are on, and over 80 per cent if it's been raining.

One thing that it is important to mention is that a leaf formed in a high-humidity environment won't ever thrive in lower humidity, so be sure that if you are growing in very high humidity, you aim to keep it that way consistently. This is why I started growing the majority of my plants without added humidity, so the environment in which they live can remain consistent for them and habitable for me, and it means you don't have to worry when you go away. I much prefer to grow them permanently at the regular house humidity, then there's no additional stress.

As mentioned on page 81, spraying or misting only improves humidity for seconds in a regular room before it returns to normal levels. Moistened gravel trays set around a plant also make little-to-no difference to the relative humidity around a plant. Grouping numbers of plants together allows their leaves to form little microclimates, but again, the effects on humidity levels are negligible. The only real way to increase humidity is to create an enclosed space within which to grow your plant, such as a cloche, terrarium, or glasshouse, or add a humidifier to your home and run it constantly – which may not be as beneficial to your home as it is to your plants!

→ Bun moss (*Leucobryum glaucum*) and *Begonia variabilis* both grow well in high humidity, which can be created under a cloche.

NAME *Corybas caudatus aff*

FAMILY Orchidaceae

GENUS Corybas

NATIVE RANGE Peninsular Malaysia

HABITAT Steep clay banks

HABIT Terrestrial

DAYTIME TEMPERATURE 15–25°C (59–77°F)

LIGHT 150–300 FC

HUMIDITY 90%+

SUBSTRATE Sphagnum moss and perlite mix

WATER Constant damp but not wet

Corybas caudatus aff

Currently the rarest plant in my collection, this is also one of the most difficult to grow, because it needs very specific conditions and the utmost stability in its environment. *Corybas caudatus aff* naturally inhabits steep, moss-covered, clay slopes in Peninsular Malaysia, which is one of the most vulnerable habitats on Earth due to the impact of climate change and habitat destruction. Since first being described, this plant has been lost to science, as there are no other records of it growing in its natural habitat and no photos or drawings. Many expeditions have failed to find it, too, so it is likely that it is now extinct in the wild, which makes successfully growing and propagating it in cultivation even more important, to safeguard its future.

The plant's natural habitat is very humid, and this is key to success when growing it in cultivation. Most attempts at growing this plant fail, but my friend Rogier manages to do so successfully in the simplest way – in bright but very diffused lighting inside a plastic sandwich bag. It always makes me smile when I see a single bag on the windowsill which happens to contain an incredibly special plant.

Terrariums

Not only do these little planters serve a practical purpose by providing myriad different environments for exotic plants in your home, terrariums can also make a really attractive decorative feature.

Terrariums are essentially transparent containers that create optimum conditions for plants to grow in, anywhere in your home. The idea of using such containers is accredited to Dr Nathaniel Bagshaw Ward, who, in 1827, was monitoring the life cycle of caterpillars in a closed jar and noticed ferns growing from the soil inside. On closer inspection he realized that these plants had grown from the spores released by the fern leaves he had placed inside the jar, which were thriving in the stable, humid environment offered by the container.

From this discovery, Ward went on to develop the Wardian case, which became a must-have item for botanists and plant-lovers alike during the Victorian era. These cases provided the ideal conditions to keep collected plants alive while being transported from more humid, tropical climes, but also created beautiful talking points in the homes of the wealthy, who could grow exotic plants in attractive containers.

Dr Ward began shipping plants all over the world in his cases, and this technique was quickly adopted by world-famous institutions such as Kew Gardens. In fact, Kew transported collected plants from all over the world using Wardian cases for nearly a century, with the last recorded instance being in 1962, when plants were brought to London from Fiji.

Modern terrariums

Wardian cases paved the way for the terrariums we see today, which are more popular than ever because they allow you to give your plants the environment they need while also keeping your environment as you prefer it. They also enable anyone the opportunity to garden indoors, no matter how small their space.

Terrariums can be either closed or open. Closed terrariums are more suitable for humidity-loving plants such as ferns, mosses, and some orchids. These are very easy to maintain because you rarely need to water them, as water vapour is trapped inside and condenses on the sides of the container before running back down into the substrate to be reused by the plants. Open terrariums can marginally increase humidity if they are tightly planted, but in general they are used more for aesthetics rather than as a benefit to plants.

You can use all sorts of objects to create these little ecosystems – from tiny test tubes to whole cabinets and even converted furniture – as long as they are watertight and transparent. Try to avoid patterned or wavy glass, though, as not only will it obstruct your view but it will also reduce the amount of light getting to the plants inside. Coloured glass also reduces available light.

The simplest terrariums can be created in a closed container, which grows lush and green in the sealed humid atmosphere, while the most complex versions are constructed in detail to recreate entire habitats on a miniature scale. If you want to try creating your own terrarium at home, see page 94 for a step-by-step guide to one approach.

Bioactive terrariums

Many terrarium guides used to call for all items used inside to be sterilized first, to avoid introducing unwanted microbes or pests. Today, people are recognizing the benefit of a less-sterile environment, and enjoying the process of creating and maintaining a bioactive terrarium instead.

The key to creating a fully functioning and self-supporting environment is to introduce insects and other critters, such as woodlice, which serve a dual purpose in cleaning up decaying plant matter and leaving behind faeces that in turn fertilizes the plants and feeds the substrate. Because of this, bioactive terrariums tend to be healthier and the plants within them often live longer. Your bug 'clean-up crew' also remove harmful microbes, and the bioactive terrarium promotes a soil structure that is teeming with beneficial microbes, which maintain a healthy environment.

Taking this approach means that the substrate, too, should not be sterilized, as you don't want to destroy the life within it; instead, you want to ensure that it has a high organic content so there is plenty for both the plants and bugs to feed on.

Watering and drainage

An important part of maintaining a terrarium is the watering. Since there are no drainage holes in your vessel you must water very carefully, keeping it to the absolute minimum – don't forget that many closed terrariums won't need much (or any) water once established because they have their own water cycle. It's also advisable to add a drainage layer of lightweight expanded clay aggregate (LECA) and then grit at the bottom of the terrarium (see page 94), beneath your chosen substrate, so there is somewhere for excess water to drain away to, to prevent root rot.

Planting

Choosing the right plants from the get-go is the difference between succeeding or not with your terrarium. Commercially available terrariums contain all sorts of plants, but make sure that the plants you choose will be happy in the atmosphere inside your terrarium and that they all require the same growing conditions – especially their water requirements. I often see succulents and cacti in terrariums, but you should avoid these. The increased humidity, lack of drainage, and airflow will surely result in rot.

Research plants that remain small and that will grow and evolve to create the right aesthetic. I love including lots of moss in my terrariums, as it grows slowly and gives a beautiful lush effect, and the plants and fauna will also root and live within it.

HOW TO MAKE A TERRARIUM

A terrarium not only provides the perfect environment for tropical, humidity-loving plants, it can also make a lovely feature in any room.

You will need Terrarium (lid optional) | Backdrop, such as bark | LECA and fine grit | Free-draining substrate | Hardscaping (logs, rocks) | Moss | Tweezers | Plants | Twine (optional)

1. Cut your backdrop to size. Here I used a cork bark panel, which will allow plants to colonize and climb on it.

2. Add a drainage layer to create an escape route for excess water. A layer of LECA followed by a layer of fine grit stops the substrate falling between larger gaps in it. Add the substrate.

3. Get your hardscaping, such as logs and rocks in before you add the plants.

4. Now add moss to the floor and hardscaping – using tweezers is easiest. You can use superglue to secure it until it takes hold. Moss can be pushed into contact with the substrate.

5. Add your plants to the substrate or moss, using tweezers if necessary to nestle them into pockets of moss. Secure them in place with pieces of twine, if needed.

6. Mist thoroughly to create a humid environment. I add a diluted fertilizer to the mister to give them an immediate boost. Leave open or close if your terrarium has a lid.

Alocasia micholitziana 'Variegata'

Although the variegated form, which is also known as Alocasia 'Frydek', is not found in the wild, its all-green counterpart is endemic to several islands in the Philippines, where it is currently threatened by habitat destruction and also over collection, due to the demand from ornamental plant growers. In cultivated plants, the variegation differs from leaf to leaf and in some plants it is more stable than in others.

In the wild, the unvariegated form, Alocasia micholitziana, grows under the canopy of other trees, however, the light it receives still equates to that of a bright spot in the home. It naturally grows in high humidity but will thrive in a home environment with no added humidity. If humidity is added, heat and airflow must also be increased to avoid problems such as rot.

NAME Alocasia micholitziana 'Variegata'

FAMILY Aracea

GENUS Alocasia

NATIVE RANGE The Philippines

HABITAT Lowland forest and secondary forest

HABIT Ground dwelling

TEMPERATURE RANGE 15–30°C (59–86°F)

LIGHT 800–1500 FC

SUBSTRATE Aroid mix

HUMIDITY 50%

WATER Damp

FERTILIZER

Fertilizing plants plays a vital part in keeping them happy and thriving – and getting their feeding needs right has a major impact on both their performance and their growth.

Why use fertilizer?

Sometimes fertilizing is forgotten about, but working it into your regular plant care will noticeably improve the growth of your plants and their overall health. I always enjoy fertilizing my plants as it feels like I'm giving them something that's going to help them out. I also know that I'll reap the rewards when I get to enjoy healthier leaves and flowers.

I use a combination of nutrient-dense substrate in my pots, with the addition of a regular fertilizer that dissolves in water, but there are many options you can choose between that will best suit your schedule and needs. Personally, I find a regular application (according to the requirements of your specific plant) really beneficial because you can monitor more closely how much fertilizer a plant is receiving and make sure that all of its nutrient needs are met. It's also no more extra work, because applying this fertilizer doubles up as a watering if you use concentrated liquid feed or dissolvable granules (see page 104). Once these have been fully dissolved in the water, the fertilizer can be poured into the substrate in the pot where it will be taken up by the plant's roots, or used as a foliar feed, where you can spray it directly onto the leaves.

Essential plant nutrients

There are several key nutrients that have different roles in our plants' development. The most important ones are N (nitrogen), P (phosphorus) and K (potassium).

Nitrogen
Nitrogen is considered one of the most important nutrients in plant growth as it is a major component in chlorophyll, which allows a plant to photosynthesize (see page 26). It's also essential for amino acids, the building blocks of the proteins that plants need to grow. The most obvious effect of nitrogen is the healthy foliage it encourages.

Phosphorus
Phosphorus is an important component in the DNA of all living things, but in plants in particular it supports healthy root growth and flower production and helps plants withstand environmental stress such as cold weather. It is particularly beneficial for young plants, helping them establish a healthy root system.

Potassium
Potassium is responsible for vital processes including water and nutrient transportation around the plant from the roots, taking it up the stems and to the leaves. This mineral also improves the drought resistance of a plant, because it works to regulate the opening and closing of the stomata – the pores on the leaves or stems of a plant. Feeding potassium to plants about to flower will also give you an abundant display.

NPK 'macronutrients' supply the majority of a plant's nutritional needs, but micronutrients are also important (vital nutrients required in lower quantities than macronutrients) for healthy growth and to boost resilience to pests and disease – particularly calcium. Plants need different amounts of each nutrient, depending on their position and time of year.

This Tradescantia grows in a small hanging basket. It needs fertilizing with almost every watering to sustain its huge size.

Houseplants are reliant on us to provide the nutrients they need. Knowing your plants, their requirements, and what products are on offer will help you choose the right fertilizers for your plants.

Choosing your fertilizer

Since I've delved deep into the array of fertilizers available and made this a part of a regular routine for plant maintenance, my indoor growing and the health of my plants has improved dramatically.

So what do you need to know in order to give your plants the best care? There are two main types of fertilizer: natural and synthetic (see opposite and page 104). (Note, I didn't say 'natural and chemical' – the word chemical is often misused when discussing synthetic fertilizers; both synthetic and natural fertilizers contain chemicals.) I'm happy to use a hybrid approach with a fertilizer that has natural

and synthetic ingredients, as this gives me the best of both – my plants get immediate access to synthetic nutrients in controlled quantities, while slower-release natural fertilizer becomes available to the plants over time.

Granular slow-release fertilizer can be added to your soil mix when repotting, which means you can forget about it for a while, or you can work more granules into the top 2.5cm (1 inch) of compost as needed. I find it hard to monitor when plants need more using this approach, so I observe them closely and take slower or smaller growth as a cue to feed.

Natural fertilizers

Made from plant, animal, or mineral materials, natural fertilizers predominantly work to stimulate beneficial microorganisms within the substrate. These microbes break down natural fertilizers and make them accessible to plants in the form of both macro- and micronutrients. This makes natural fertilizers slow-release, as although some of these nutrients are immediately available to your plant in small quantities, most are only accessible with the help of these microbes. The microbes perform best when the substrate isn't too wet or too dry and is at a stable temperature, so pots exposed to a lot of sun and prolonged dry periods may have a lower microbe activity. Repeated use of pesticides and chemicals will destroy these beneficial microbes, which in turn makes the growing medium sterile.

Of the various natural fertilizers on offer, dried seaweed is one that I'm a big fan of. It contains myriad micronutrients and works wonders on plants. I find fertilizers with added seaweed give all the benefits of a natural fertilizer but without the smell of some others, such as chicken manure.

Another effective natural fertilizer is a living compost made from decomposed sheep's wool and composted bracken. This also makes a fantastic topdressing (see page 110) for plants that just need a little pick-me-up and aren't quite ready for a full repot. Applying a thin layer of this on top of the substrate one or two times a year or when the soil level drops in the pot or becomes dry and dusty acts as a wonderful slow-release fertilizer. Use the topdressing alone or add other components to create your perfect substrate mix (see page 58).

If you are using a natural fertilizer, be aware that the higher the organic content in your substrate, the more likely you are to attract fungus gnats (see page 158), because they feed on the fungus growth. While they won't damage your plant they are a real nuisance buzzing around your home, so avoid excess nutrients by not applying too much.

PROS

- Slow-release
- Long-lasting impact
- Promotes substrate health
- Improves substrate texture
- Less likely to cause fertilizer burn on plants

CONS

- Can attract fungus gnats
- Slow for plants to absorb
- Reliant on temperature and environment to be effective
- Can smell or be messier to use because many types don't come in neat packaging

Synthetic fertilizers

These are artificial products created using gases in the air and processed minerals. Synthetic fertilizers are available in a wide range of application methods – from powder and granules to liquid forms. All of these can be mixed into substrate or added to water in a solution that can then be added to the growing medium or used as a foliar feed (see page 108).

Some growers find that one advantage of using synthetic fertilizers is that the nutrients are accessible to the plants without the need for microbes in the substrate to first break them down. Because of this, the fertilizers get to work quickly in supporting a plant's growth and overall health, although in general they do very little to improve soil health or structure, which can in turn impact the health of the plant's roots.

Synthetic fertilizers can be manufactured in volume and you know exactly how much of each nutrient you are applying to your plants because the ratio is clearly marked on the packaging. This makes it easy to monitor your usage. If you follow the guidelines on the packaging and flush your plants regularly to remove any nutrient and salt build-up (see page 109), you can prevent burning of roots and leaves.

My preferred form of synthetic fertilizer is dissolvable granules used either to water the soil or as a foliar feed. This is a very cost-effective method as there is less wastage – and anything in my plant care that combines two jobs (watering and fertilizing) is a winner in my eyes!

↑ Synthetic fertilizers allow plants immediate access to nutrients.

PROS

- Easy to store, because they always come in packaging, unlike some natural fertilizers
- No mess or smell
- Rapidly absorbed by plants
- Consistent nutrients in a product

CONS

- Doesn't add to soil biodiversity
- Overuse is more likely to cause fertilizer burn
- Mostly has a short-term effect
- Requires more frequent applications

My favourite fertilizer mix

Fertilizer packaging – whether natural or synthetic – in the garden centre will list the major components of the mix, most often including NPK (nitrogen, phosphorus, and potassium, see page 101).

In general, most houseplant varieties are happy being fed using a 20–10–20 ratio – which means it contains 20 per cent nitrogen, 10 per cent phosphorus, and 20 per cent potassium. However, each plant and growing environment is unique, and some require different N-P-K ratios or concentrations to thrive. This is why getting to know your plants is important so that you can take their lead on how often to apply fertilizer.

I use a hybrid fertilizer of natural and synthetic fertilizers that I created myself. I now have it professionally made, so it is also available for customers in my shop. I add in a little seaweed extract, too, which provides all the micronutrients that are required by indoor plants for overall health, and also promotes soil microbiology.

Another wonderous product that I add into the mix is fulvic acid, which is made when microorganisms in soil break down. It's a bio stimulant, which means that it provides a food source for beneficial microorganisms and helps to make micronutrients more readily accessible to a plant's roots. It also supports soil health and structure and encourages beneficial microbes. Another huge benefit of fulvic acid is that it improves your plant's drought tolerance, meaning it will suffer less damage if you forget to water it or are away from home for a short period.

For most plants, I use my favourite mix, dissolving 5g (1 teaspoon) of fertilizer into 4.5L (500fl oz) of water.

NAME *Anthurium veitchii* x *chamberlainii aff*

FAMILY Araceae

GENUS Anthurium

NATIVE RANGE Chamberlainii – endemic Venezuela; Veitchii – Colombia

HABITAT Mountain forest

HABIT Epiphytic

TEMPERATURE RANGE 18–30°C (65–86°F)

LIGHT 500–1500 FC

SUBSTRATE Bark chips or sphagnum moss

HUMIDITY 50%

WATER Evenly damp; substrate can be dry between waterings

Anthurium veitchii x chamberlainii aff

A hybrid of two *Anthurium* species – *Anthurium chamberlainii* and *Anthurium veitchii*, this plant has a leaf form that combines beautiful characteristics from both parents. New leaves emerge with a deep, blood-red colouring that indicates the presence of anthocyanins – coloured pigments – which deter predators and help protect new growth from sun damage.

    Anthurium chamberlainii was first described in 1888 and has only been recorded once more since. The exact location of the species is still a mystery. *A. veitchii* (see page 31) is epiphytic, so it's important to use a very well-draining substrate. I use sphagnum moss to top the substrate in terracotta pots to allow for plenty of surface evaporation. I hadn't seen this plant flower, so I use a high-nitrogen and potash feed to support large leaf growth and encourage flowering. If you are not using an aroid flower for propagation, I'd usually remove it as it hinders leaf growth – but this one is too beautiful to cut off.

Fertilizing should be a part of your plants' regular maintenance. While it is important to fertilize all year round, you should balance this with the growth of your plants and their growing position.

Using fertilizer

How you use your fertilizer depends not only on the type of feed you are using, but also the particular plants you are feeding, as well as the time of year – for example, if they are dormant or in full growth. Whether you use natural or synthetic fertilizers is a personal choice; or, like me, you can opt for a hybrid approach and create your own mix (see page 105).

Including fertilizing in your regular plant care – for example, adding fertilizer when watering and as a foliar feed – keeps it simple, but the frequency of doing this depends on the plant. Getting to know your plants' individual needs is vital to get this right, so that your plant gets enough nutrients to thrive and grow healthily, but not so much that it can cause problems (see overfertilizing, opposite).

Routine and care

Fertilizing should be a key consideration in regular care for potted plants. I fertilize the majority of my plants on one watering, then use plain water on the next. This routine works really well in controlling the amount of fertilizer applied so that you don't overfertilize (see opposite).

Some plants, such as cacti and orchids require a more tailored regime (see pages 114 and 111), and most carnivorous plants do not require any extra nutrients at all.

Remember, if your plants are having a growth spurt they will require more nutrients, which is why it is important to fertilize plants in pots almost all year round in the recommended quantities. However, in winter, if growth slows or a plant is dormant, reduce feeding. The basic rule is to adjust feeding in line with growth; I recommend every other watering because the amount of water your plant uses usually reflects the rate of growth.

Keep it fresh

A common trend is to sterilize growing medium before using it in pots by rinsing it with boiling water or drying it out in a low-temperature oven. This can be done to kill any pests and minimize the chances of introducing unwanted critters into the home. However, the disadvantage here is that this also kills beneficial microbes, leaving the substrate barren and thus unable to do its important job of breaking down natural fertilizer for our plants. I prefer not to sterilize substrate and instead promote a balanced ecosystem by encouraging beneficial microbes.

Overfertilizing

While fertilizer is invaluable in growing healthy, happy plants, too much of a good thing can cause damage.

Overfertilizing can be catastrophic for a plant because it causes root burn, which happens when the salt levels in the pot become too high and draw water out of the plant, preventing it absorbing water.

A telltale sign of overfertilizing is a browning or 'scorching' on the edges of leaves and stunted, weak growth of the plant in general. If you tip the plant out of the pot you will see browning on the roots, too.

Overfertilizing happens when certain nutrients build up inside the pot, causing what's known as a 'nutrient lock', which makes it impossible for other nutrients to be absorbed and thus the plant becomes starved. To prevent this, always follow the manufacturer's instructions on the packaging of your fertilizer to achieve the correct balance of nutrients. Never think that adding more and more fertilizer will necessarily equal more growth. You will only cause more damage to your plant.

Another way to control the nutrient level in your soil is to flush the pot through with clean water between fertilizing, each time allowing the water to fully drain out of the pot's holes. This will remove any excess salt in the substrate and prevent nutrients building up to a dangerous level.

TOPDRESSING

Adding a thin layer of fresh compost on top of the existing substrate in the pot is a fantastic way to add nutrients naturally while also improving soil structure and aiding moisture retention. It is also perfect for a plant that needs a little TLC but isn't ready for a full repot.

You will need: Plant in pot | Substrate (I prefer an aroid mix for this)

FERTILIZER

1. Prepare your substrate in your preferred combination. I like to use my usual aroid mix (see page 58). Get this ready in advance so you can apply it straight onto any exposed roots.

2. Gently start scraping away the top 2.5–5cm (1–2 inches) of loose substrate from your pot with your hand. Remove and either add to your compost bin or mix it up with new compost to refresh it and use elsewhere.

3. Apply a thick layer of your topdressing mix to the pot, making sure you cover all the exposed roots and that it settles at the same level as before.

4. Water thoroughly to settle the topdressing and to start allowing the nutrients within it to work their way through the substrate, down to the roots.

Orchids

While orchids require a little feeding, any fertilizer that is applied should be diluted to a lower concentration than for other houseplants, because orchids require fewer nutrients and a too-concentrated fertilizer will burn their roots (see page 109). I water my orchids last, after I've fed all my other plants, by leaving around a quarter of the fertilizer solution in the watering can that I have made up for my other plants, then topping it up with just water. This mix is at a quarter of the strength and perfect for most orchids.

Orchids such as Phalaenopsis grow and flower all year around, so these should get a high-nitrogen and potassium feed every other watering, to support good leaf growth and flowering. Other orchids grow seasonally, so throughout the growing season a fertilizer higher in nitrogen will support leaf growth, while switching to one higher in potassium as they enter flowering season will give you the most bountiful blooms.

To fertilize your orchid, dissolve the fertilizer in water and pour into the pots, allowing it to flush through. Gently shake the pot to remove excess water and allow it to drain before returning it to a display pot, to avoid water building up and causing root rot. Orchids also respond well to a foliar feed splashed or sprayed over the leaves.

Phalaenopsis orchid care

These orchids are a huge success story. They have been the gateway plant for many collectors and can be found relatively inexpensively anywhere from specialist growers to supermarkets. However, this accessibility also makes them botanical 'fast fashion'; there is a big environmental impact if they are simply thrown away after flowering, and there is a temptation to do just that and replace them with another plant in flower. But with the right care, Phalaenopsis can re-flower for many years. My oldest plant is one of these orchids, which was given to me by my nana for my sixteenth birthday and it is still going strong, flowering beautifully, like clockwork, as the temperatures start to drop as we head into the winter months.

→ Misting Phalaenopsis with a diluted fertilizer is a great way to apply feed.

NAME *Bulbophyllum lobbii*

FAMILY Orchidaceae

GENUS Bulbophyllum

NATIVE RANGE From India southwards
to Thailand, the Philippines, and Malaysia

HABITAT A wide range of forest
and jungle

HABIT Epiphytic

TEMPERATURE RANGE 15–30°C
(59–86°F)

LIGHT 500–1500 FC

SUBSTRATE Bark chips

HUMIDITY 65%+

WATER Leave to dry
between waterings

Bulbophyllum lobbii

This fascinating plant has a flower that looks almost insect-like, with a hinged lower lip that moves in the breeze. Most Bulbophyllum are pollinated by flies and produce a floral secretion that acts as a food reward to pollinating insects, but in contrast to many others in the family, *Bulbophyllum lobbii* releases a beautiful floral scent that's similar to jasmine and orange blossom.

These orchids require bright light but need to be shaded from direct sun during the majority of the day. To fertilize, use a specialist orchid feed or dilute your other houseplant fertilizer to a quarter strength. A nitrogen-rich feed will support the formation of new leaves and pseudobulbs (the thick, fleshy, bulb-like structures you can see above), which hold water and nutrients. These pseudobulbs are where the flowers will emerge, so to encourage flowering, a potash-rich fertilizer is recommended during winter and into spring and early summer when they flower.

Cacti

Cacti live in very harsh environments and are adapted perfectly to survive and thrive with limited water and nutrients. To allow them to grow at their healthiest we need to try to mirror these environments in our homes. Of course, light is the most important factor, with cacti requiring very high light levels. However, alongside light, it is important that the substrate mix is very free-draining, to avoid water sitting in the pot and leading to rot. This is because their succulent, water-filled bodies can decay quickly if they are left in wet conditions for too long.

Despite the popular belief that cacti only need a tiny amount of watering at a time, if their growing conditions are right it is much better to water them thoroughly less often than allow them to completely dry out between waterings. Soil can become hydrophobic – it repels water – if it is bone dry, but adding enough sand and grit into the mix can help prevent this and makes it easier to re-wet it.

All of the cacti growers I've spoken to have a very different fertilizing routine, but one idea they all share is to use a fertilizer with a lower amount of nitrogen but with higher phosphorous and potassium. This is because too much nitrogen can cause faster, weaker growth which is softer and more likely to collapse or rot.

For the first year there is adequate nutrition in a freshly repotted cacti, and after this regular fertilizing will support healthy growth and flowering. Fertilizing every other watering is a good schedule, but be sure to use a specialist cacti food or dilute another houseplant food further than you would for your other plants. A quarter to half the strength of normal solution will avoid overfertilizing.

Cacti often have tough appearances that reflect the harsh conditions in which they live; clockwise from top: *Ariocarpus retusus* v. *confusus, Lophophora williamsii, Geohintonia mexicana, Aztekium hintonii, Strombocactus disciformis, Pelecyphora strobiliformis.*

NAME *Geohintonia mexicana*

FAMILY Cactaceae

GENUS Geohintonia

NATIVE RANGE Mexico (Nuevo Leon: Sierra Madre)

HABITAT Gypsum cliff face

HABIT Terrestrial

TEMPERATURE RANGE 10–35°C (50–95°F)

LIGHT 2000 FC

SUBSTRATE Free-draining mix of grit, sand, pumice, or molar clay with less than 10% organic content (compost, etc.)

HUMIDITY <60%

WATER When completely dry and only when nighttime temperatures are consistently above 10°C (50°F)

Geohintonia mexicana

The appearance of this very rare and fascinating plant perfectly shows its adaptations to the harsh environment in which it lives. It is endemic to only one area of approximately 25km (15.5 miles) and lives on sheer gypsum cliffs with little to no rainfall. These harsh conditions, with minimal water and nutrition, means it grows very slowly and even when mature it is only a few inches tall. To get it to look how it does naturally in our homes we must provide it with those same conditions. Too much water, nitrogen, or a lack of light will create a taller plant with an 'unnatural' look. It is definitely better to underfertilize than over, and some growers don't fertilize it at all but most feed it in early spring to promote flowering and continue to feed during summer intermittently.

Its native population was almost wiped out by collectors, and it is listed in CITES appendix 2 – the list of species whose trade must be controlled to ensure their survival in the wild – so when buying do so responsibly to avoid plants being poached.

Fungus support

Over recent years mycorrhizal fungi have become buzz words amongst outdoor gardeners, and I've heard whispers among indoor growers, too. It's an area I'd like to explore further, as this fungus is vital for our plants, to improve their nutrient uptake, and I see huge potential to improve the health of our plants. These fungi are apparent in living soil, but many substrates for pots are sterilized, so these won't contain the fungi, and some plants have a partnership with a specific type of fungi, which is not necessarily going to be present in a chosen substrate mix. So, for these reasons, potted plants will benefit from a little added sprinkle.

Mycorrhizal fungi live quietly in the soil, where they influence water absorption as well as nutrient and mineral uptake, meaning they not only support your plants' growth but also its drought tolerance and resistance to pests and disease. These fungi are associated with over 90 per cent of the roots of all plant species and have a unique relationship that benefits themselves as well as the plant. They create vast webs throughout the soil, acting as an extension to the plants' own root system, transporting nutrients and water back to the roots. While the fungi support the plant in its growth, the plant provides the fungi with sugars to enable it to survive and reproduce.

We can add mychorrhizal fungi in powder form to the roots of cuttings during transplanting or on the outside roots of plants during repotting. Doing this will help your plants create their own unique support system, which will help them establish faster and minimize transplant shock.

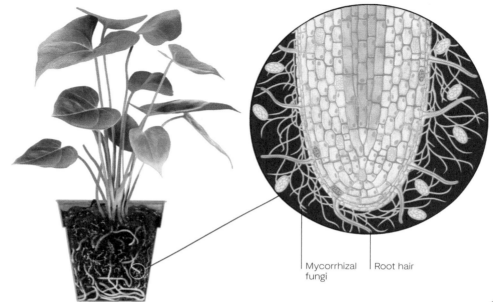

Mycorrhizal
fungi

Root hair

Mycorrhizas are beneficial fungi that grow around the root system of a plant, transporting water and nutrients to the plant, and thus extending its absorptive reach.

→ Applying mycorrhizal fungi is an easy job, and one that enables plants to establish quickly.

PROPAGATION

Propagation is a simple and inexpensive way to bolster your collection of plants and varieties. From just one plant you can create multiple new clones of your favourite specimen, or even exciting new hybrids. There are myriad ways by which you can do this, depending on the species of plant.

Propagation techniques

Propagation is my favourite part of tending plants; not only does it create new plants, but growing them from the very start of their existence gives you a level of understanding of them that can't be achieved in any other way. Witnessing the first roots and leaves emerge and watching how they develop is invaluable to learning about how best to care for them.

Reproducing your existing collection of plants and swelling their numbers also gives you more plants with which you can experiment without risking losing your parent plant. I love to trial how changes in light, substrate, and other conditions

affect plants' growth. Sometimes these investigations work and sometimes they don't, but each one helps me to improve as a grower. Everything I learn can then be shared with other plant enthusiasts – and vice versa. Propagating is also a fantastic way to get more of your favourite plants for free, not just to enjoy yourself, but also to give to friends or even sell on in your own cottage industry.

There are multiple methods you can use – some very straightforward, others needing a little precision – depending on the plant you want to propagate. But most of these you can do at home.

NAME *Begonia darthvaderiana* x *malachosticta*

FAMILY Begoniaceae

GENUS Begonia

NATIVE RANGE Cultivated hybrid

HABITAT Shaded rainforest floor

HABIT Ground dwelling

TEMPERATURE RANGE 18–25°C (65–77°F)

LIGHT 100–200 FC

SUBSTRATE Sphagnum moss or akadama

HUMIDITY 90%+

WATER Damp but free-draining soil

Begonia darthvaderiana
x *malachosticta*

This dramatic cultivated hybrid has been created from *Begonia darthvaderiana*, which was documented in Kalimantan, Borneo, in 2013, and *Begonia malachosticta*, which originates in Sabah, Borneo. Both species require very specific growing conditions that the hybrid also needs to grow well, but the right care will reward you with dark spotted leaves as it matures, which lend themselves to leaf cuttings (see page 123).

Both begonias require a very high humidity of 90 per cent, and I grow mine at 100 per cent humidity in a greenhouse, or you can use a cloche (see page 89). At this humidity, it is important to have a substrate that remains damp but allows airflow and prevents water building up in the pot, because the plant is very susceptible to rot and 'melting' – where it literally disintegrates before your eyes. *Begonia darthvaderiana* grow naturally in the understorey of the jungle, so avoid bright light on their delicate leaves as this will cause significant damage.

Leaf cuttings

Propagating certain plants from leaf cuttings is a truly fascinating process. In the wild, some species have evolved so they can propagate new plants from their leaves if the parent plant is damaged. So when broken leaves land on the forest floor, instead of just rotting, they will grow on as clones.

One great aspect of leaf propagation is that you can propagate many new plants from just one leaf. You can also group multiple cuttings in one pot or tray initially, to make efficient use of space.

Begonia and Streptocarpus are perfect plants to propagate from leaf cuttings, but they do need very high humidity to get started, so a propagator or even a little glass jar is ideal. For leaf cuttings, plastic pots are more suitable than terracotta because they are better at retaining much-needed moisture. If you want to try this with your plants, on the opposite page there is a step-by-step guide to propagating from leaf cuttings.

↑ Begonias can be propagated in individual pots or in trays with many different plants.

PROPAGATE BY LEAF CUTTING

Using a begonia as an example, here's how you can create several new plants from just one leaf, while keeping your mother plant looking fresh and balanced!

You will need Blade or snippers | Fungicide | Root stimulator | Live sphagnum moss 10cm (4in) plastic pot | Tray | Propagator or jar

1. Select a good-sized leaf, avoiding older ones that have started to deteriorate or newer, softer ones more likely to rot. Cut the leaf away from the plant at the petiole (leaf stalk).

2. Lay the leaf on its front and either make tiny incisions across the veins or cut all the way through the leaf to create multiple strips. Try to keep the leaf's shape, to ensure you lay its underside onto the substrate.

3. Sprinkle a fungicide and root stimulator over all the cuts you have made – this is not essential, but it helps the delicate leaves to root quickly and avoid rotting.

4. Add the moss and a sprinkling of fungicide, and root stimulator to the pot. Push the petiole of an intact leaf into the moss; plant leaf strips (see step 2) underside down on the moss.

5. Place the potted leaf (or strips) into a tray lined with moss and place it inside a heated propagator – a humidity level of 90–100 per cent with adequate airflow is ideal.

6. After a couple of weeks the leaf will start to root and new plants should emerge along the leaf veins. Carefully trim these away and pot on separately once they've grown new leaves.

Stem cuttings

Most houseplants can be propagated relatively easily using this method, and taking stem cuttings will result in exact copies of the mother plant.

I take cuttings from my own mother plants, but I always make sure I have other back-up plants ready to take their place, because consistent cutting over time does cause their quality to degrade. So only use healthy material and try to cut in the cooler part of the day to ensure the resulting cutting is fully hydrated. Something I always do is to give my plant a good drink and feed a day or two before I take cuttings from them.

Once you've taken your cutting, it is important to follow up with regular care and attention, to ensure a healthy new plant. Using a substrate that is moisture-retentive but free-draining will keep your cutting hydrated and helps to avoid rot (see page 87). I always prefer to pot up cuttings in terracotta containers, as this is a porous material that allows airflow around the base of the cutting. Increased heat, humidity, and sufficient light (see pages 88 and 24) will ensure your cutting roots quickly and gets established swiftly. To generate enough heat to get a cutting started, you could use a propagator, but you don't need one. Instead, place the plants inside a large, transparent storage box, and add a heat pad if the ambient room temperature isn't over 20°C (68°F) – you can buy these pads from any reptile supplies store.

A prepared cutting of *Rhaphidophora tetrasperma* 'Variegata'.

PROPAGATE BY STEM CUTTING

Stem cuttings are a great way to create new plants from old, and it's really simple to do. This can be done at any time of year when the mother plant has suitable healthy stems to snip from.

You will need Sharp, sterilized blade, such as secateurs | Terracotta pot or seed tray Live sphagnum moss | Propagator

1. Select a healthy single node (a shoot including leaf, petiole, and stem with an axillary bud – a bud in the joint between stem and petiole). Cut below the leaf joint, leaving some stem you can trim higher up if it rots.

2. Next, cut away the top half of the leaf by laying it on a flat surface. Doing this lowers the amount of water lost by the cutting and allows the plant to generate new growth much more efficiently.

3. Fill a terracotta pot or seed tray with sphagnum moss and place the node flat on top. If a cutting has aerial roots, I bury them but leave the node exposed.

4. Place the container and cutting in a propagator heated to 25–30°C (77–86°F) during the day, 10°C (18°F) cooler at night, to stimulate rapid root production.

5. A new leaf will emerge before roots. Once your plant has roots, acclimatize it to life outside the propagator by gradually uncovering it for increasingly lengthy periods.

6. Once the cutting has hardened off you will be able to transfer it to its final growing position.

NAME *Alocasia melo*

FAMILY Aracaea

GENUS Alocasia

NATIVE RANGE Sabah, Borneo

HABITAT Rocky, damp terrain

HABIT Upright

TEMPERATURE RANGE 25–30°C (77–86°F)

LIGHT 400–800 FC

SUBSTRATE Coarse aroid mix

HUMIDITY 60%+

WATER Keep soil evenly damp

Alocasia melo

A wonderfully tactile plant, *A. melo* has one of the most miraculous leaf textures – it is deeply veined and feels rough and fleshy to the touch. The plant originates from the jungles of Sabah, Borneo, where unfortunately, like many plants in the region, its numbers are declining. However, you can propagate your own plant by harvesting tubers, and it has also now been tissue cultured (see page 135) and is available in cultivated form. Hopefully this will help to safeguard the future of this unique and beautiful plant. In the wild it has been found growing in a more rocky terrain than many varieties of Alocasia, so although *A. melo* likes to be damp in its native habitat, avoid leaving it sitting in water, keep its soil mix open and airy, and allow it to totally dry out between waterings.

A. melo thrives in very high humidity (see page 88 for growing tips), when it produces less-distorted leaves, a level of humidity that can be achieved in glasshouses but can be more difficult to reach in the home. The foliage colour changes drastically with light levels, turning from pale steel-grey in partial shade to green in direct light.

Tubers

Tuberous plants such as Alocasia, begonias, and some members of the ginger family give us two options for propagating. One is to cut into and divide the tuber of the parent plant, while the other is to harvest the small tubers that the plant naturally creates throughout the soil in its pot.

In the wild, roots will travel away from the parent plant and at the end of these roots small tubers will start to form, which, once they reach a suitable size, will grow into a new plant. This allows plants such as Alocasia to spread and colonize areas in its natural habitat, creating great swathes of foliage.

Cutting into the tuber (see page 129) may seem rather scary to some, so you might prefer to stick to the less-invasive method of tuber harvesting. Both these techniques are detailed on the following pages for you to try, but whichever one you use, each offers a great way to multiply your plants for free while still retaining the parent plant.

Tubers of *Alocasia melo* ready to harvest.

The excitement of hunting for new tubers amongst the plant roots in a pot gives me so much joy. You never know what – or even if – you will find anything, but when you do, plucking that tuber from the substrate feels like the ultimate reward for your care of that plant. It's also a fairly non-invasive way to multiply your Alocasia collection.

You will need Jar or food container, with a lid | Live sphagnum moss

1. First search the surface of the substrate – often an Alocasia will push new tubers to the top of the pot.

2. Gently turn your pot upside down, using your hand to cover the top, and slide out the rootball. A little squeeze on the sides of the pot or a tap on the base will help to loosen it.

3. Pluck out any detached tubers around the rootball with your fingers. For any tubers stubbornly attached to a root, a little twist will free them.

4. Clean any substrate away from the tubers with water (you can do this in the sink or over a bowl).

5. Leaving space at the top of the jar, place an inch or two of damp sphagnum moss in the base of your jar. The tubers will sit on top of this, a couple of inches apart. Do not bury them.

6. Place a lid on the jar and pop it somewhere very warm (30°C/86°F). To harden off a well-rooted plant, open the lid for short, but increasing, periods of time.

TAKING A TUBER CUTTING

Don't be intimidated by this technique – it's easy when you know how. This method can be used at any time of year but it works particularly well when the plant is dormant, usually in the winter months.

You will need Sterilized sharp secateurs or blade | 10cm (4in) terracotta pot | Substrate (I prefer an aroid mix for this) | Propagator

1. Carefully tip the plant out of its pot and gently scrape away the substrate attached to the tuber to expose it.

2. Cut the top off the tuber, which will have the current leaves growing from it.

3. The remaining tuber can be sliced into multiple pieces, but make sure each disc has at least one eye – this is the small bump where new growth emerges.

4. Leave the cut pieces on a dry surface for several hours to callous over and dry.

5. Plant each tuber in its own pot of substrate, to the depth it was planted originally. Some plants, like Alocasia, don't like to be disturbed, so having their own pot avoids repotting later.

6. Place in a propagator at 25°C (77°F) with ventilation to prevent the tuber rotting. Once its roots fill the existing container, transfer to a pot one size larger to prevent shock.

Pollination and seed production

This is one of the most common methods of propagation, and is how I first learned about plant biology, but it's often overlooked in cultivating houseplants. This is probably because we rarely grow these plants just for their flowers, especially aroids.

Aroids are interesting because the inflorescence (flowers) on various species can differ. Some are hermaphrodite (each flower is both male and female), while some have male and female flowers on the same spadix (flower spike). In most cases, the flowers are surrounded by a leaf-like bract called a spathe, which in turn surrounds a spadix, containing the male and female flowers. The female flowers typically open first to avoid self-pollination from the pollen in the male flowers above. Most flowering plants are hermaphrodites that can self-pollinate.

For pollination to occur in plants that contain both male and female flowers on one spadix, the spathe opens to allow pollinators in once the female flowers are receptive. Visiting insects may carry the pollen from the male flower of another plant, thus pollinating the female flower as they enter. On many plants, the inside of the spathe is slippery and closes to keep the pollinators inside during the night. This gives the best chance of pollination and gives pollinators the perfect environment in which to breed themselves.

Once the female flowers are no longer receptive the male flowers start to produce pollen and the spathe opens again. As the pollinators begin to climb up the spadix to leave the plant they brush past the male flowers, picking up pollen, which they then carry to another plant in the female stage.

In order to improve their chances of reproduction, different plant species have evolved fascinating tactics to attract specific pollinators; some use scent, colour, and even heat (see thermogenesis, opposite) to lure in the pollinator that is most likely to pollinate them successfully.

If you want to try this at home, you can store the pollen from a male flower in the freezer and wait for the next female flower to be receptive. Then, when the moment comes, transfer the pollen to the receptive female flowers using a fine paintbrush or your fingers. It's a good idea to stagger your applications to increase your chances of a successful pollination.

PROPAGATION

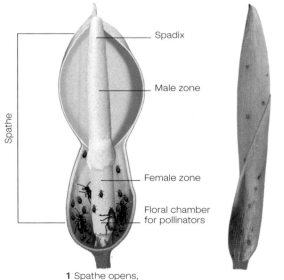

Spadix

Male zone

Spathe

Female zone

Floral chamber for pollinators

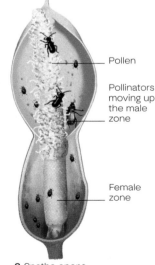

Pollen

Pollinators moving up the male zone

Female zone

1 Spathe opens, female receptive

2 Spathe closed

3 Spathe opens, female no longer receptive

← Illustration showing the male and female stages of a *Philodendron spiritus-sancti* inflorescence.

↑ *Amorphophallus titanum*, or corpse flower in full bloom is stunning if rather smelly...

Thermogenesis

One clever adaptation to attract plants is a method of heat production, known as thermogenesis. This process was first described by naturalist Jean-Baptiste Lamarck in 1778, when he witnessed the inflorescence of an *Arum italicum* beginning to increase in temperature. Thermogenesis in combination with scent is used to target specific pollinators, to ensure particular insects visit the same species, thus limiting the amount of hybrids produced by cross-pollination of species and improving the likelihood of successful pollination. The heat the plant emanates carries the scent of the inflorescence, which acts as a beacon that can be detected across the jungle understorey by pollinators. That heat also mimics the heat released by decaying meat or fruit.

This fascinating process can be vastly different amongst species; some heat minimally over a very short or longer time, while others increase the temperature of the spathe by 35°C (60°F) or more above air temperature.

Perhaps the most famous instance of thermogenesis can be seen in *Amorphophallus titanum*, which has the world's largest unbranched inflorescence, at over 3m (10ft) high. It is known as the corpse flower because it releases a charming scent of rotting flesh, which appeals to flies and carrion beetles.

Amorphophallus titanum has both male and female flowers on one inflorescence, with the female flowers near the base opening first. During female flowering the entire spadix heats in waves, with temperatures peaking around 36°C (97°F). After flowering the spadix cools and the male flowers bloom. Thermogenesis is used during male flowering, but slightly differently. Instead of the spadix heating up, the individual male flowers heat to attract pollinators to collect pollen.

NAME *Anthurium warocqueanum*

FAMILY Aracaea

GENUS Anthurium

NATIVE RANGE Colombia

HABITAT Lowland rainforests

HABIT Epiphyte

TEMPERATURE RANGE
15–30°C (59–86°F)

LIGHT 500–1000 FC

SUBSTRATE Bark chips or
sphagnum moss

HUMIDITY 90%+

WATER Just damp and can dry
between waterings

Anthurium warocqueanum

Also known as 'The Queen Anthurium', it's not hard to see how this Colombian beauty earned such a name. Its velvet leaves can reach huge proportions, and the way they emerge is fascinating. Each leaf first appears as a fully formed but soft, tiny leaf, then over the following weeks it gradually swells and begins to harden and present its unmistakeable trademark matt-velvet and endlessly tactile leaf. The most effective way to propagate this plant is through pollination using its own pollen or that of another *A. warocqueanum*. The seeds can then be harvested and sown (see page 134), with the leaves increasing in size by around one-third with each new emerging leaf. I grow mine in a greenhouse in pure sphagnum moss in terracotta pots, which works very well, and I fertilize with every other watering, or with each watering while a new leaf is being formed.

HARVESTING AND SOWING SEED

Although harvesting seed sounds complicated, it is actually another really simple method of propagation that requires minimal equipment and can easily be done at home.

You will need Snippers | Receptacle (bowl or jar) | Bowl of water | Seed tray with lid
Damp sphagnum moss | Pots | Propagator

1. If pollination was successful, the base of the inflorescence (the flower) on your plant will swell. Once swollen and the berries are ripe, remove it with snippers.

2. Use your hand to gently start removing the inflorescence and collect the seeds in a bowl.

3. Pour the seeds into a bowl of water, then squash them a little to separate the flesh from the seed casings.

4. Transfer the seeds to another bowl – as you do so the flesh will pour away, leaving the seeds behind.

5. There will be a lot of seeds, so it is better to sow them into a tray filled with moss rather than individual pots. Lay the seeds on the surface, cover, and place somewhere warm and bright.

6. When the seedlings have two or three leaves they can be potted up individually into more containers of sphagnum moss and grown in a propagator until they each have 4–5 leaves.

Tissue culture

Quite simply a cloning technique, tissue culture, or micropropagation, is the practice of growing plants in a laboratory using their cells. The cells are grown in a sterile, artificial environment in optimal conditions to encourage them to divide and form new plants. This method is used to produce the majority of houseplants sold today.

Some mutations in plants, such as variegation (see page 140), are valued by collectors, but in commercial cultivation the aim is to produce consistent batches of plants with minimal mutations. The tissue culture process allows thousands of plants to be grown across a batch with consistency in a much shorter time and with fewer resources.

In order to do this, a 'protocol' is established for the production of each plant, which allows the growers to reproduce cells efficiently and at the best quality. Different

chemicals and hormones are used in varying quantities to encourage particular cells to multiply at different times. Initially, the protocol for each variety will produce more mutations, but over time and through experimentation this protocol is tweaked. Ultimately the goal is to get mutations that have a positive impact on cells and produce healthier, more robust plants.

Plants propagated by tissue culture vary greatly in quality depending on the mother plants used for the donor tissue and the protocol. A perfectly sterile environment is also essential to avoid contamination from possible microbes and diseases, which is why this process is conducted in laboratories.

When buying tissue-culture plants, make the usual checks (see page 17), but also avoid very small specimens or those still in their lab flasks, unless you are experienced in cultivating them. Without the right care, the risk of these plants dying is very high.

NAME *Philodendron spiritus-sancti*

FAMILY Aracaea

GENUS Philodendron

NATIVE RANG Espirito Santo, Brazil

HABITAT Tropical forests

HABIT Hemiepiphytic

TEMPERATURE RANGE 25–30°C (77–86°F)

LIGHT 500–1500 FC

SUBSTRATE Bark chips or sphagnum moss

HUMIDITY 50–80%

WATER Constant damp substrate

Philodendron spiritus-sancti

One of the few plants in the world that has more plants in cultivation than in the wild. Currently listed as endangered, the locality of this very rare plant is limited to one very small area of Espírito Santo, in Brazil, resulting in minimal genetic diversity. Luckily, the plant has made it into cultivation, where it can be propagated, although the process is notoriously difficult and not something most of us can try. Recently its pollination in cultivation has been documented for the first time, and plants have also been reproduced through tissue culture (see page 135). This is a great example of ex-situ conservation, where the plant is conserved outside of its natural habitat with the hope of being reintroduced to the wild one day.

Because of its rarity, *P. spiritus-sancti* is sometimes the victim of too much TLC. It's a tough plant, and although a relatively slow grower it is far happier under- than overwatered. *P. spiritus-sancti* is a hemiepiphyte (it spends part of its life cycle growing on other plants), so it will not tolerate its roots standing in water. It grows most aesthetically with light all around or overhead.

VARIEGATION

Patterned and coloured plants demand attention amongst a sea
of plain foliage. How plants achieve this variegation is a fascinating process
that you can aid them with once you understand it, with only
a little specialist care.

Understanding variegation

Put simply, variegation is a variation in pattern or colour, and it can be a really special feature of plants' leaves, stems, flowers, or even roots. The different causes for these variations are key to understanding specific plants and how best to care for them.

In the plant world, there are two distinct schools of thought about variegation: one is in favour of variegated plants, the other against them. Some people feel that these are rather garish, unattractive or – for a few purists – that they look like diseased plants that are more difficult to care for than their green-only counterparts. Others, like me, love them and want to celebrate their uniqueness in all their forms.

Variegation occurs naturally in the wild; one example is the *Aglaonema pictum* 'Tricolor', which has stable genetic variegation (see opposite) that is thought to have evolved to help it blend into the shady jungle floor in Sumatra. Genetic mutations can either occur as a result of stable genetic mutations, or chimeric, or are caused by other influences, such as viruses (see pages 145 and 148).

Five plants of interest
Philodendron hastatum 'Variegata'
Philodendron spiritus-sancti 'Variegata'
Philodendron mamei 'Variegata'
Alocasia amazonica 'Variegata'
Rhaphidophora foraminifera 'Variegata'

Stable genetic variegation

Also known as 'pattern-gene', this type of variegation is caused by specific genetic information within the plant that creates a pattern (or patterns) of different colours. Although this is common in the wild, the reason why plants have evolved in this way is under much debate. Some people believe that this variegation evolved to resemble pest or disease damage, in an adaptation designed to deter other predators from attacking the plant; while others think it's simply a form of camouflage. In reality, both of these arguments could easily be true.

For the plant enthusiast, not only are genetically variegated plants interesting to grow, they also offer the opportunity to create new and exciting hybrids and cultivars that can be bred specifically for visual appeal. As genetic information is constant, this form of variegation is fully stable; therefore, most such plants will produce clones of the mother plant when propagated either by seed or vegetation.

With the exception of botanically rare or protected species, plants with stable genetic variegation never reach dizzying heights of desirability amongst collectors, because supply and demand for them can be easily met.

The variegation in *Aglaonema pictum* 'Tricolor' gives it a camouflage-like foliage.

Aglaonema pictum 'Tricolor'

Prized for its incredible camouflage-style foliage, Aglaonema pictum 'Tricolor' has been heavily poached in Sumatra to feed the insatiable appetite for its beauty. It grows in the jungle understorey in lower light, but in nature this is much brighter than most would consider low light to be in their home. It will survive in 100 FC or less, but to thrive, a minimum of 200 FC is necessary. High humidity of 70 per cent+ is beneficial, although I've seen several specimens grow well in a home environment with a 50/60 per cent humidity.

A. pictum 'Tricolor' will readily flower, especially when stressed or given a high-potash feed. If you want to expand your collection, inflorescences can be pollinated (see page 130); the seeds usually have a great success rate (see page 134). Plants can also be propagated as clones through stem cuttings or division when growths emerge around the mother plant (see page 124).

NAME Aglaonema pictum 'Tricolor'

FAMILY Araceae

GENUS Aglaonema

NATIVE RANGE Sumatra

HABITAT Jungle understorey

HABIT Terrestrial

TEMPERATURE RANGE 20–34°C (68–93°F)

LIGHT 200–500 FC

SUBSTRATE Bark chips or sphagnum moss

HUMIDITY 70%+

WATER Just damp and can dry between waterings

VARIEGATION

↑ *Philodendron gloriosum* 'Variegata' has very unstable chimeric variegation.

Chimeral variegation

This form of variegation occurs in plants that have two chromosomal make-ups, wherein some cells produce chlorophyll and others do not. Leaves can appear in a multitude of shades of green, white, and yellow, and can change in colour, pattern, and appearance from one leaf to the next.

Such instability poses a challenge for even the most experienced gardener, as it makes these plants unpredictable to propagate and means they require more specialist care.

Chimeral variegation is rarely seen in the wild through natural selection, because such plants would be outcompeted by their non-variegated counterparts. However, new research suggests that variegation in some plants may in fact offer evolutionary benefits, such as having a better tolerance to colder temperatures or to create protection from herbivores. As herbivores don't see in colour, the suggestion is that variegation, and its difference in tones and contrast, are more camouflaged to their eyes, which could help a plant to better blend in with the rest of the jungle and avoid being eaten.

The emergence of chimeras is also usually a game of numbers, and since such huge volumes of plants are grown in cultivation, this makes it more likely that these chimeras will pop up. Traditionally, oddities like chimeral variegation were destroyed in commercial cultivation because there was value in uniformity. Fast-forward to the present day, and the scarcity of desirable variegation and the challenges faced by propagation means that there is a huge market worldwide for these unique beauties – in fact, these plants can fetch six-figure sums from the most enthusiastic buyers.

Blister or reflective variegation

Blister variegation occurs naturally in many forest-floor-dwelling plants. The effect is created by a small air pocket under the epidermis (the outermost cell layer), which reflects light for a silver appearance.

There are many theories around why this variegation has evolved. One idea is that it improves light absorption for the plant, while others think the differences in colour work as camouflage to protect plants from herbivores, or to mimic insect damage so other pests don't stop by for a snack.

Interestingly, many blister-variegated plants lose their variegation as they begin to climb into the canopy when they grow in the wild. If you want to see how these plants morph into their adult forms as they climb, give them something to scramble up right away – a wooden board, moss pole, or even a wall will do. If you want to continue the characteristics of blister variegation, you can propagate new plants through cuttings or by seed (see pages 123, 125, and 134).

NAME *Rhaphidophora tetrasperma* 'Variegata'

FAMILY Aracea

GENUS Rhaphidophora

NATIVE RANGE Southern Thailand and Malaysia

HABITAT Tropical jungle

HABIT Climber

TEMPERATURE RANGE 15–28°C (59–82°F)

LIGHT 500–1000 FC

SUBSTRATE Sphagnum moss or aroid mix

HUMIDITY 60%+

WATER Damp

Rhaphidophora tetrasperma 'Variegata'

While the non-variegated *Rhaphidophora tetrasperma* is common in the wild and in cultivation, a variegated version has never been found in its natural habitat, likely due to natural selection. This plant's chimeral variegation (opposite) is either caused by a random mutation or through tissue culture (see page 135). In the majority of plants this variegation is incredibly unstable and can't be relied upon to come through, but some mother plants are more stable.

Rhaphidophora tetrasperma 'Variegata' is easy to grow but needs care to do well. For the substrate, use sphagnum moss or an aroid mix with bark, organic compost, and bracken, which will retain moisture and drain well. Keep evenly damp at all times; if the substrate dries out the white leaf cells will absorb water too quickly, then rupture and turn brown when watered. A temperature higher than the optimum range of 15–28°C (59–82°F) results in rapid softer growth that is more likely to brown. When potting up, use a wide pot to give the plant room to grow, and allow space for a moss or bark pole (see page 67) for it to climb and develop mature leaves with fenestrations (see page 36).

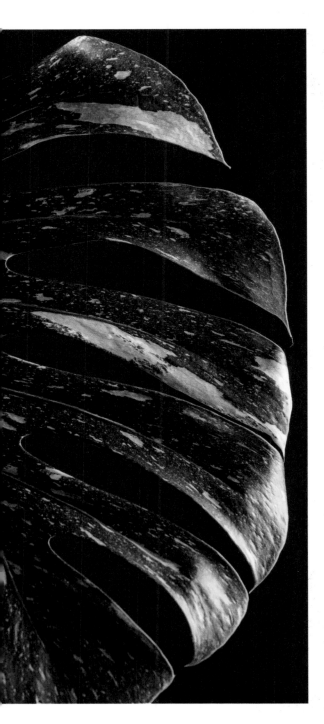

Induced variegation

Variegation can be induced in plants in several ways under laboratory conditions, resulting in either a permanent genetic mutation, chimeral variegation, or a temporary variegation. It's a very common practice and is being used to create new cultivars for the market, but it's not often spoken about.

Sometimes variegation is induced deliberately, while at other times it happens as a result of other processes, such as tissue culture (see page 135). During tissue culture a large volume of plants are created, which increases the likelihood of mutations, but the process and the chemicals used also increases the rate at which mutations occur.

The main method of inducing variegation is through mutations; plants and cells can be subjected to chemicals, radioactivity, and other external aggressors to encourage these to occur. The resulting mutations can cause many different outcomes in a plant's growth or look – variegation being just one of these – but any that emerge and have desirable traits will be kept and grown on in the plants.

Viruses are also used in the creation of new cultivars – sometimes unknowingly but also sometimes very deliberately. The word virus strikes fear into many, but often they can be present in a plant and remain inside it with little to no detrimental effect and not ever lead to a damaging disease. The most famous example of a virus in cultivation was during the seventeenth-century Tulip Mania, where one flower infected with a virus commanded huge sums of money due to the mutations caused by it. Today there are many notable plants, including some camellia and viola species, that present very attractive variegations as a result of a virus.

Monstera 'Thai Constellation' is a reliably stable variegation; this form could have come about by inducing mutations in *Monstera deliciosa*.

Evolving variegation

Variegation can and does change in many plants, and while traditionally chimeral variegation was seen as a defect in plants, it's now not only valued by collectors, but research is showing that these mutations can actually have a benefit to some plants. For example, during one study it was discovered that a wild plant with a white chimeral variegation had a greater cold tolerance to its non-variegated counterpart. The theory was tested extensively under varying growing conditions and all results showed the same conclusion.

There is limited reliable information available on the effects of light on variegation, and my general thinking – along with most others in the houseplant world – was that chimeral variegation couldn't be changed and it was completely random. However, during deeper research for this book I discovered several studies citing the impact of light on variegation in several different genera of plants. Specimens were grown under varying light conditions and the resulting changes in level of visible leaf variegation were monitored. The results showed a conclusive increase in variegation in the plants grown under a higher intensity of light.

A fascinating study undertaken by scientists at the University of Florida on communication between a mother plant and daughter plantlets used changes in variegation to illustrate how the mother plants seem to communicate with plantlets that are on their attached runners – or stolons, as they are known. In this study, the mother plants and their offspring were exposed first to the same light levels and then to differing levels; sometimes the mother received higher light levels and other times the offspring did. What is interesting is that when the mother plant was in a higher light level than her offspring, she became greener and there was a decreased level of variegation, even though a higher light level should increase variegation. This not only suggests that the mother plant and her plantlets communicate, but it clearly shows a change in variegation that is influenced by light.

From this we can see that it is possible to change variegation in some plants using light and heat. What I will say, too, is that each plant is completely different, so they will react to changes in temperature and light differently. Some variegation may increase as light levels increase; some could decrease. Similar results could be shown with changes in temperature and some plants may not change at all, even with a changing environment.

The only way to learn more about our plants is to experiment, and if you give this a go, try to do it with several plants under controlled conditions, only changing one variable at a time, so you can see whether this and this alone brings about changes.

Reversion

Reversion – when a plant reverts to its green form and loses variegation – can happen in variegated plants, and it is fairly commonplace in some that have unstable chimeric variegation. It can be incredibly disheartening to see the beautiful variegated plant you bought and carefully cultivated begin to revert to its all-green form. Sometimes this just happens, even when there is no change in the external environment, but there are some things you can do to bring back variegation to your plant. I'm currently in a variegated battle with a *Philodendron* 'Golden Dragon'. I will premise this with the fact that this beautiful plant is terribly unstable and known to revert a lot – especially when it is cut for propagation. So don't invest in one unless you are happy to be left with an all-green plant, but when you do get variegation, it is, in my opinion, unbeatable. I think that's where part of its appeal lies. It's a constant challenge.

The first thing I'd recommend when faced with a reverted plant is to leave it. Sometimes variegated plants will give you many green leaves, then randomly start throwing out beautiful variegation again. This is exactly what my 'Golden Dragon' has done; several green leaves later it produced a beautifully variegated leaf. I'm glad I resisted cutting it.

If you have recently moved the plant there could be a link between the change in environmental factors and the change in variegation. Continue to monitor it, then maybe move it back to its former spot after allowing several new leaves to grow while in its new location.

Variegated *Philodendron* 'Golden Dragon' is highly unstable.
Here you can see all-green foliage (right), variegated white (left)
and a leaf in the process of variegating (centre).

We tend to choose variegated plants precisely for their often unique or fascinating appearance, but to keep these plants looking their best, they need a little bit of specialist care.

Caring for variegated plants

Many aspects of variegated plant care are similar to those you would follow with non-variegated plants. However, there are some areas where some different care is needed – particularly for white and yellow, more sectoral variegation (those that have large patches of white on the leaf).

The main consideration when growing variegated plants is ensuring the stability of their environment. Many variegated plants will be negatively impacted by large fluctuations in light, humidity, and watering, and in these situations may revert to their all-green form or experience browning or decay of the variegated parts. So to keep them looking at their beautiful best, you need to give them as much stability as possible.

Light

It is chlorophyll that gives plants their green colour and allows them to photosynthesize and produce energy. In white, paler-green, or yellow variegated plants the absence or lower levels of chlorophyll means that the plant doesn't have the same capacity to photosynthesize, and because of this, it's even more important to make sure variegated plants get enough light. Care must be taken with the leaves, though, because variegated parts of plants can burn more easily. Being in direct sun for a couple of hours a day during the morning or late afternoon is fine, but avoid leaving these plants in direct sun during the hottest parts of the day. Overall, a longer amount of less-intense light is preferable.

Humidity

Although most variegated plants come from very high-humidity environments, I've found adapting them gradually to a lower humidity can be very beneficial in the longer term. Large patches of white and yellow variegation are susceptible to browning, and a high humidity can create the perfect atmosphere for some of the fungus that can cause this. If you do choose to grow at a higher humidity, it's important to also increase the heat of the growing area and ensure there is good airflow around the plants to help negate the problem.

Watering

Consistency with watering is more important for variegated plants that have larger pieces of sectoral variegation. Avoid letting the substrate dry out completely, as the white parts of the leaf are less drought-tolerant, so that when you do water, the rapid influx of water can rupture the delicate cells. This results in browning of the leaves and excess guttation (see page 86), the latter of which releases water from the tip of the leaf to create a constant wet environment that is perfect for fungus to take hold.

→ A gorgeous trio from left to right: *Tradescantia zebrina* 'Quadricolor', variegated *Monstera lechleriana*, variegated *Philodendron billietiae*.

PESTS & DISEASES

My own feelings about pests have changed drastically over the last few years. A few years ago I thought full extermination of all pests was the way to achieve perfect plants, but I now know I was completely wrong.

Managing pests

Working with plants outdoors helped me to understand the link between a healthy ecosystem and a healthy garden, and to embrace the fact that plants are one small part of a much wider ecosystem.

As a result, I quickly left all pesticides behind in favour of creating a diverse ecosystem in which pest predators thrived. Removing chemicals led to healthier soil, full of beneficial microbes, which in turn created a better soil structure and made nutrients more available to my plants. I was rewarded with stronger, healthier growth that was more resistant to both pests and diseases.

Learning to live with pests has to mean accepting they are inevitable. I don't aim to wipe out all pests but to manage their numbers to keep them at a level that doesn't cause my plants significant damage. This also means accepting that plants are not designed to be perfect, and striving for immaculate leaves will always lead to disappointment in the long term, as it isn't achievable. My focus is on overall plant health, making sure they receive optimum light levels, nutrition, and watering so they can defend themselves against and be minimally affected by pests.

Prevention

When we think about pest control it's usually in terms of the physical removal and treatment when the problem has already occurred, but for best results it should start well before this, through establishing optimum plant health and good housekeeping practices.

Although at some point you will have to focus on managing the pests amongst your plant collection, you should also try to prevent some new pests arriving and the situation getting out of hand. Controlling the levels of existing pests to a degree that doesn't cause damage to your plants' health is key to winning the battle.

One way of managing pests is to examine new plants thoroughly before you bring them home and introduce them to your other plants. Two great pieces of kit to help with this are a white piece of paper and a lint roller. You can place the paper under any plant in a shop or when you get it home, then give it a shake and you may see some dislodged pests falling onto it. For large-leafed plants you can use a lint roller if you prefer – gently roll it over the undersides and tops of leaves, then you can examine anything that it removes.

When bringing new plants into your collection, even if you've thoroughly checked them over, put them in another room away from your plants for around two weeks. During this quarantine period, keep checking on them for any signs of pests, but also make sure the new plants are receiving all the other usual care you would give your plants and an optimal environment to help them settle into their new home.

→ Using a lint roller is a fast and effective way to find and remove pests.

Pests

Forewarned is forearmed, so here is a run down of the most common pests that you might encounter on your houseplants.

A pest is anything that can cause damage to your plant, but how much damage they cause and how much of a pest they become is usually down to early, consistent and effective management. They can become tiresome and a frustrating nuisance, but only if you choose to see them that way.

Thrips

Probably the most common pest seen in houseplants, these tiny insects can multiply rapidly and if left unchecked can cause significant damage. Most adults are 1–2mm long and can be anything from a pale brown to almost black in colour. They are usually found living on the leaf and its underside, sometimes tucked tightly against leaf veins to avoid being seen.

A thrip's life cycle follows five main stages: egg, larval, prepupal, pupal, and adult. The female inserts an egg into the soft tissue of a plant's leaves, fruits, and flowers, where the eggs hatch into larvae and begin to feed on the plant by piercing plant cells and sucking their contents. This leaves the telltale spotting and tracks across a leaf where the cells begin to die after a thrip has fed. The adults also feed in this way.

Once the larvae reach the next level of maturity they pupate and either remain on the plant or drop into the growing medium before emerging as adults. Thrips can enter your collection on new plants, on your clothing, on fresh produce like fruit and vegetables, or even just through an open window; so being thrip-free indefinitely is near impossible.

Aphids

There are more than 5,000 described aphid species worldwide, which can also be known as greenfly, blackfly, or whitefly, although they come in whole range of colours. They are usually 1–7mm in length and are found predominantly on the new-growth tips of plants, which makes them easy to spot and

control. Aphids multiply rapidly, with wingless females giving birth to live young that quickly colonize plants. Aphids at all life stages secrete a sticky honeydew that can also attract moulds to grow on plants, so it's a good idea to remove any affected parts of the plant after you deal with the pests, to decrease the risk of any further issues developing.

Spider mites

You will likely notice the spider mites' damage before you see the sap-sucking insects themselves, which thrive on plants in a dry atmosphere like our homes. These yellowish-green mites often leave telltale signs, such as speckling across leaves, white cast skins, and egg shells. In heavier attacks leaves will begin to pale and have stunted growth. You may also notice the mites' signature webbing across the leaf or at the leaf base where it joins the petiole. These tiny things are only 0.5mm in size, but can cause significant damage to leaves and may weaken and kill entire plants if left unchecked, so regular and consistent maintenance is needed.

Fungus gnats

These are those tiny but highly irritating flies that are more of a nuisance to us than a threat to our plants. Adult flies are 3–4mm long and feed on fungus and dead and decaying organic matter in soil. They lay their eggs in damp substrate and the larvae hatch out into maggots, which also feed throughout the substrate. They will cause no harm to established plants but they may munch on the tender growth of seedlings or cuttings and damage plants if their numbers are high. However, practising good all-round care and maintenance will prevent the numbers escalating.

Mealybugs

Mealybugs live on the leaves and stems of plants, particularly in the cracks and crevices of leaf axels and inaccessible parts of the plant, but there are also some species that affect the roots. Mealybugs don't tend to travel far, so control is fairly easy, especially if you avoid bringing them into your collection on new plants. I've only had mealybugs once and that was on a cutting of a mature *Monstera* 'Thai Constellation', which has ample hiding places. The creatures moved to the plant next door, but after a few days of consistent searching and physical removal they were gone.

Root mealies can be more of a problem as they usually go undetected; the only way you discover them is when your plant is already showing signs of distress. Looking at the roots, you will be able to spot them as fluffy white spots of wax, but the damage can be quite significant by then.

Scale

Evident as hard domes that are about 1–3mm in size that appear on your plants' leaves and stems, these are in fact the sedentary adults, which are protecting the eggs. Once hatched the nymphs crawl and begin to infest new plants, feeding on their sap. Many species secrete a honeydew that can cause moulds to develop. Plants can appear weakened and have yellowing leaves, which should be removed, and a severe infestation can cause leaf drop.

Pest treatment

When we say the words 'pest treatment' the first thing that springs to mind is the array of available pesticides on offer to tackle the problem, but it's my strong belief that we must move away from these. I haven't used pesticides outdoors for many years, but I was using them indoors until a year ago, when I fully realized their devastating effect on the environment, aquatic life, beneficial insects, and bees.

There are both natural and synthetic pesticide options available on the market. If you choose to use natural products, remember that they should be used with the same respect and caution as synthetic options, as natural does not necessarily mean safe. In addition, always use a product that has been formulated for use as a pesticide and has been licensed as such, because these will include guidelines to keep you safe. Avoid all unlicensed products, which can be sold

illegally in many countries, but especially those pesticides that claim to be 'green' or 'environmentally friendly'. It is most likely that they are neither.

To manage pests, my preferred approach is physical removal. As I said earlier, my aim is never total elimination of every pest from my collection – that would be impossible or would need the use of a lot of toxic chemicals because of the amount of plants I have. Also, because I live in the middle of the countryside and need to keep my windows open during the summer to prevent the place overheating, pests are continually arriving through the open windows from outside.

When I'm checking my plants and I come across pests I'll use my fingers to remove or squash them. If the plant has a larger number, I'll take it into the shower or out into the garden for a good hose down. This will dislodge many persistent pests, and I can then follow up with a wipe-down with a clean microfibre cloth to sweep away remaining creatures.

This is the method I use consistently as general maintenance, which I see just like any other care task – like watering or pruning. I check my plants over for pests every couple of weeks, but if I see numbers increasing on certain specimens I'll up my frequency to weekly to stop the spread. However, it's rare that I have larger numbers appearing, because in the absence of pesticides I get help in controlling pests from other insects and spiders who will devour them.

Even though we don't have the same ecosystem inside our homes as we do outdoors, we can step in to be our own biological control and hopefully get a little bit of support from other insects already living inside. If you have fewer plants it would be easy to totally irradicate pests using this method alone, then just keep up the maintenance regularly to avoid new outbreaks going unnoticed.

Diseases will occur on your plants from time to time, and their severity can range from unsightly to fatal. As with pests, good maintenance and prompt action will keep your plants healthy.

Managing diseases

Plant diseases can be abiotic (non-infectious) or infectious. Non-infectious diseases are often caused by factors such as nutrient deficiency or poor air quality; infectious diseases are caused by bacteria, fungi, or viruses. Although plants can be affected and damaged by bacterial diseases, good plant care minimizes the risk of most taking hold and killing the plants. As well as diseases, viruses can also cause significant problems, and unfortunately there's no effective treatment for these. But if you know what to look out for, you can prevent viruses spreading amongst the other plants in your collection.

Root rot

This has to be one of the most common diseases in houseplants. It's usually caused by the substrate being too wet for too long, which provides the perfect environment for the fungus that causes root rot to develop and take hold. Root rot is usually identified late; the roots may be significantly damaged before a plant shows any visible effects. The signs to look out for are drooping leaves and stems – as if the plant is underwatered – and a still-damp substrate. This is because the rotten roots are not able to take the available water up into the plant. Leaves may also start to degrade, with brown or black tips. When you check the roots, they will be brown, black, and mushy and may also have a putrid smell as opposed to the white, firm roots of a healthy specimen (see page 87).

Fungal leaf spot

This disease is why I advise against misting in home environments, but fungal leaf spot can occur without misting, too. It appears on leaves as small brown spots that sometimes have a yellow centre or ring, and can quickly spread across leaves and throughout whole plants in its preferred conditions. This can occur anywhere, but cool damp environments and standing water on leaves can amplify the risk. Plants do benefit from being placed together in groups but the humid, still environment with little airflow that this can create is ideal for fungus to thrive.

Sooty mould

This is easily identifiable on an affected plant and usually occurs when there is a pest at work. Insects like aphids and mealybugs secrete a honeydew; this attracts ants, which eat it and in return protect the aphids from other predators. This honeydew is also the perfect breeding ground for sooty mould. As its name suggests, sooty mould is black, powdery, but sticky, and can appear anywhere on a plant's leaves. It is mostly concentrated in areas where pests have been feeding.

Powdery mildew

This white, fine powdery fungus can develop and coat any part of the plant. It thrives in cool, damp environments where plants are densely packed. This is often fairly mild if it is spotted and treated early, by removing and destroying any infected parts. Good drainage and air circulation will help prevent infection.

Bacterial leaf spot

As the name suggests, this causes water-soaked spots that soften the leaf tissue. This usually takes hold in cramped or poorly ventilated conditions; in a wet atmosphere these spots run together to create mushy sections, whereas in drier conditions these spots will dry out. The wet leaves can appear more translucent or black, while the dry spots take on a reddish-brown hue.

Disease treatment

Diseases will appear in any collection, but good housekeeping and husbandry can really minimize the chances of occurrence. Creating good airflow around plants, especially those that live in a high-humidity environment, and not misting leaves in places with low airflow means you remove the conditions that the bacteria and fungus thrive in. Removing any dead or diseased leaves and pruning plants so they are not too dense also really helps. As ever, getting my plants to optimal health is always my main focus, alongside prevention, then if diseases strike, the plant has the best chance to fight these off with minimal damage.

Viruses

Houseplants are susceptible to many viruses, and some can be circulating throughout collections without us knowing, because they have little or no impact on growth or the visible health of the plant. Others, though, can be devastating.

Viruses have no available treatment, so unfortunately plants that are badly afflicted must either be destroyed or completely segregated from other healthy specimens. Any propagation of these plants will also result in new plants being affected by the same virus.

Biting and sucking insects such as thrips (see page 158), will spread viruses, but another common way by which they are spread is through propagation. If an infected plant is cut and that blade is then used on another plant, it can transfer the virus to it. This can be a real problem in commercial cultivation, because the number of plants being propagated by cuttings can make the likelihood of spreading viruses more likely.

Although viruses in houseplants are rare, they do happen and one of the most common is the mosaic virus family. These cause distorted growth and a telltale mosaic pattern throughout the leaves.

Philodendron 'Jose Buono'

This plant is a botanical mystery, because its origins are unknown and as yet, we don't know whether it's a hybrid or a cultivar, or where the original plant or parent plants came from. Philodendron are native to tropical America, and so we give it the same care we would give to other plants in the genus that come rom a similar habitat. I've had great success growing it in my greenhouse and in my home, and although it grows faster with higher heat and humidity, its thick waxy leaves allow it to adapt beautifully to home conditions and lower humidity. The plant will grow bigger if it is given a pole or surface to climb. The one pictured is just about to be mounted onto a moss pole, although I definitely prefer them at this height and in a pot like this, so I may take a stem cutting from it, then repot that into another pot. I'll then have two plants to enjoy.

NAME *Philodendron* 'Jose Buono'

FAMILY Aracaea

GENUS Philodendron

NATIVE RANGE Unknown

HABITAT Unknown

HABIT Climber

TEMPERATURE RANGE 20–30°C (68–86°F)

LIGHT 800–1500 FC

SUBSTRATE Sphagnum moss or chunky aroid mix

HUMIDITY 50%+

WATER Allow to dry between waterings

Extrafloral nectaries

When you think of nectaries, people tend to think of those found within a plant's inflorescence that secrete a sweet nectar to attract pollinators such as insects or birds. Extrafloral nectaries, however, occur outside the flower, on the stems and leaves of over 100 plant families across the globe. They can be seen as very small drops of nectar and can be confused with pest damage, but look closer and don't panic, as it's completely healthy and natural for your plants to do this. *Philodendron* seem to show the most obvious extrafloral nectaries, which are particularly visible on new growth.

In the wild, extrafloral nectaries attract ants and other aggressive arthropods – but not for pollination. Instead, by offering ants a sweet nectar, the plant encourages them to live nearby, creating a symbiotic relationship; the ants acting as a natural pest control by killing or deterring pests such as caterpillars and other herbivores, which might otherwise damage the plant.

Fascinatingly, although plants with extrafloral nectaries come from all over the world and myriad habitats – from jungles to deserts – with vastly different morphologies, the extrafloral nectar itself is remarkably similar across all plants that exhibit this process. Usually, nectar found in flowers differs from plant to plant, as its job is to attract specific pollinators for that specific plant to avoid cross-pollination between species, but in extrafloral nectaries the nectar is designed to attract mainly ants, which means it must be similar across species.

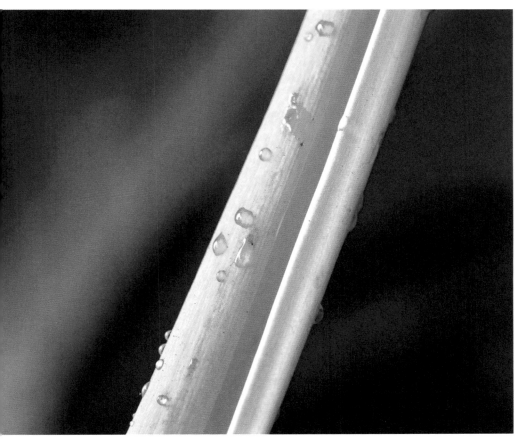

The nectar from extrafloral nectaries visible
on a *Philodendron billietiae*.

RESPONSIBLE GROWING

Understanding the history and the origins of our houseplants gives us a deeper appreciation of where they come from and how they came to feature in our homes.

A brief history of plant exploration

Our passion for rare plants is steeped in history – for centuries people have travelled the globe in the name of science to find and document 'new' plants and take them back to their own countries. For the most part these explorers were collectors and botanists from wealthy countries who travelled to colonies far away from their own shores. While wider science of course benefitted, the chief purpose of many of these explorations was to find plants that were commercially viable and that could be grown in the explorer's homeland or throughout other colonies.

Unfortunately, much of this research was undertaken with brutality and little respect for the Indigenous peoples or habitats in which they were discovered. Slavery was also part of these explorations, with enslaved people used aboard ships or on the plantations that grew vast monocultures of the plants that had value. On top of human exploitation, this culture often destroyed natural habitats, with vast swathes of fertile ground cleared for crop cultivation – often with no thought to wildlife and plants – and rare and endangered species stolen without care of extinction.

The origin of plant names

The pillaged plants were documented as new discoveries by explorers, and in naming them the botanists included little or no acknowledgment of the Indigenous peoples, who had cultivated a deep understanding of their biology and uses over generations. Sometimes knowledge was collected from locals about certain plants, but once it was passed on, these Indigenous people were erased from the narrative in favour of the botanists who 'discovered' the plants.

The recording of these 'discoveries' has also caused another problem – in plant nomenclature. Botanical Latin is used to describe plants around the world and is important as a consistent language recognized and used internationally. However, even though historically many of the plants that were documented already had names that gave information about how it could be used or where it grew, some were completely erased and not referenced in the 'new' name or description. Instead, often the names included a reference to the botanist recording the plant, who snuck it in for posterity. Botanical names can contain clues of a plant's origin, its family and give indications of its morphology, where it grows, and a wide range of other information.

Righting the future

While we can't undo the damage caused by our predecessors, we can try to right some of their wrongs and acknowledge the people and places where the plants originate.

There are also other things we can all do to ensure we are enjoying our plants but not at the expense of others. We must stay open and curious to change and ensure that we garden and collect plants more responsibly.

There are a lot of fantastic resources to explore, from people with a lot more knowledge and understanding than me who freely share this information online.

Artists travelled with early botanists to record in colourful detail whatever was found.

On our threatened planet, it is up to us to protect rare species in sustainable ways – to respect the people and the habitats of their countries of origin, and to nurture these plants with preservation and the environment in mind.

A modern approach to botany

Modern-day issues within horticulture may no longer include such abhorrent practices as slavery, but the quest to find ever more rare and interesting plants is still problematic. Removing rare species from their habitats has an impact not only on our planet and its biodiversity, but also the people and the economies that depend upon these plants. On the other hand, many laws make the legal collecting of plants difficult or impossible.

With the climate crisis worsening all across the globe and its effects becoming more obvious, it is vital for the future of our planet that we all work together to lessen our impact on the environment. Buying and cultivating plants – whether indoors or outdoors – can play a part in this, from sourcing them, to their care and cultivation, and even to their disposal.

We should all strive to grow our houseplants with these considerations in mind, and it is easy to do if you are willing to make a few enquiries about your plants.

So, here are a few issues to be aware of when buying and growing houseplants, and the best practices we can follow to avoid harming our delicate planet.

Poaching

Mention poaching and most people think about animals, but this activity is prolific in the world of plants, too, and it can have devastating consequences. Many of the rarer plants we love to collect are endemic to very small areas in the world where even minimal poaching can completely eradicate the entire population of a plant – and with it a whole ecosystem. This is because plants are often food sources for insects and mammals or offer cover or breeding ground to others, thus the removal of a single species can have serious effects on multiple layers of the food chain, which can in turn affect whole ecosystems.

Poaching isn't confined to rare plants, it also includes many of our favourite, more common houseplants. In order to prevent the spread of pests and diseases, there are regulations that stop, limit, or add significant expense to transporting plants around the world. This in turn means that despite some cultivated plants being widely available, it is too expensive or complicated for traders to import them, but therefore easier and cheaper for unscrupulous dealers to just remove them from the wild and smuggle them out.

This is, of course, a very difficult conversation to navigate, because even without illegal poaching, all plants were at some point taken from the wild. However, it is important that botanists conduct their work responsibly for future discoveries, to ensure plants – particularly rare species – can continue to grow and have a place in their natural habitats.

Ideally, I'd like to see seeds or small numbers of plants taken from the wild by locals, then multiplied in cultivation to satisfy the global demand without further removal of more plants. The issue lies with the huge demand and fast-paced trends in plants, and in order to satisfy these, plants are poached.

I'd also be very keen for botanical collections to be propagated in cultivation and freely shared. This would mean a greater number of plants could be grown in a more responsible way and genetics spread around the planet, further protecting these plants.

→ Many species of Alocasia are in cultivation, but importation red tape means they are still poached from the wild.

How to source responsibly

I do everything I can to avoid buying poached plants – and by this I mean plants taken directly from the wild and sold on. Dealing with other growers and collectors who you know have propagated the plants in cultivation is one way to avoid this, and I rarely import plants from their native country. In addition, I will only buy from verified sources with a trusted reputation and who I know collect their specimens responsibly and with no damage to the wild plants or the wider ecosystem, or I swap plants with other collectors, using plants that I have propagated myself.

So how do you know if your plant has come from a responsible source? One clear sign is that often plants taken from the wild have a lot of leaf damage. This is because plants that have grown outside in their natural habitat are subject to pest, disease, and environmental damage and so they are a world away from cultivated plants in their appearance.

Ask your supplier about where their plants have come from. Many plants are now tissue cultured in vast quantities (see page 135). Although this is a manufactured form of propagation, the advantage of this is that it enables consumer demands to be met at a lower price to the purchaser. This in turn means there is less incentive for poachers to take those plants from the wild if the market for them is already well-stocked.

↑ The majority of houseplants are grown en masse from tissue culture, but rarer plants may not be available.

Horticulture to benefit local economies

I've seen first-hand the economic benefits that plant cultivation can bring around the globe, especially in South East Asia and South America. The Philodendron above was growing in the gardens of Ecuagenera, in Ecuador, a farm that produces rare plants in volume for sale and export. This is just one example of how families and even entire villages have been able to build an industry that can offer jobs to locals within the business of cultivating and selling of plants. When done responsibly, plants can offer a wide range of jobs from growing and propagating to packing, shipping, and promotion across social media to access a global audience. The key here is that it's the local people who benefit.

Many subsidiary industries can also emerge from the world's fascination with houseplants. I had a fantastic trip through the Andes and the Amazon basin with a guide who had an innate understanding of the local ecosystem and plants that you could only have by living amongst them, as he had, and a knowledge handed down from past generations. This is the sort of knowledge that must be protected and also shared, so as not to lose it in the future.

↑ We were driving through the Amazon and our guide pulled over to show us this wall of plants containing many natural hybrids. Seeing the plants in the wild has inspired how I grow and display them, and has given me pointers for their care.

↑ I created this cutting wall in my shop. Customers bring in a cutting and swap it with something that's already there.

Growing responsibly

Growing plants is often seen as a very 'green' thing to do, but like many products they take a huge amount of energy and resources to produce, which can have a huge environmental impact.

Many large-scale growers have implemented technology and growing techniques to minimize their impact on the environment, such as using geothermal energy to heat greenhouses, solar power to supply electricity and lighting, and even harvesting rainwater from the expansive glass roofs of their greenhouses. This water can be circulated and reused, minimizing the amount of wastewater and avoiding taking water from the grid. There is an incentive here, too, as waste in commercial growing equals less profit, so many of the systems in place are extremely economically and environmentally efficient.

What can we do?

While domestic growing doesn't involve the same carbon footprint as commercial growing, it's important to consider what we can all do to minimize our own impact while still enjoying growing plants.

Overconsumption of plants is a big issue. It's so easy to get overexcited when you see all these incredible plants, and you can end up carrying home huge numbers of them. But large collections are an enormous amount of work, and the more plants you have, the more limited your time and resources become, and plants can suffer. This leads to another issue – many people give up and throw away their plants, and in a similar way to the world of fast fashion, the low price of some plants means that if it doesn't look perfect – or in the case of orchids or other flowering plants – stops flowering, it's not such a wrench to just chuck them away and replace them.

So it's important to value your plants – buy plants you know you have time to look after, regularly assess your collection, and rehome rather than throw away things that don't bring you joy or fit into your growing conditions. In my shop I have a zero plant-waste policy; any plants not looking their best are sold at a discount with the necessary advice to perk them up, or I'll take them home and do it myself.

If you are ready and able to increase your collection, propagate from your own plants rather than buying more, and share plants with others. I've got a wall in my shop where people can swap cuttings. This removes the need to buy plants and encourages a sharing and propagation culture, while also building a community of like-minded, passionate plant people. I really recommend finding or even starting a group and getting swapping.

Make considerate adaptations

Try to use substrates that are the least environmentally damaging (see pages 54 and 55) and reuse when repotting (see page 59). Unless the plant potted in it was diseased, just mix in fresh ingredients to add structure, nutrition, and life to existing substrate instead of throwing it out. Many traditional substrates and additives have a huge environmental cost and aren't sustainable, so reusing these will greatly reduce your gardening footprint.

Recycling takes a huge amount of input, which can end up more damaging to the environment, so buy fewer things of a higher quality. These will last many years and reduce your impact on the environment and be more cost-effective in the long term. Good-quality tools last a lifetime and can be passed down the generations rather than buying something of lower quality that needs replacing every year. The same goes for pots; so many pots and trays are made from flimsy plastic which lasts a season, and most can't even be recycled. Much better to invest in some really sturdy plastic pots which will last a lifetime.

I propagate and then grow many of the plants for my shop on windowsills at home, with no additional light or heat needed.

Being part of a plant-loving community has great advantages, including sharing advice on how best to grow your plants. However, there is also some advice out there that isn't always based in fact. Here are a few of my favourite myths.

Myth Busting

Myth: Plants clean the air

Not a day goes by without hearing someone claim that plants 'clean' the air. A 1989 study by NASA into methods to clean air in sealed environments such as the International Space Station is often used to corroborate these claims. The results of their tests suggested that plants absorb carbon dioxide and release oxygen, while removing some pollutants from the air. However, the experiment didn't show that houseplants can clean the air in our homes, just that plants (or the substrate they are in) can remove certain chemicals from the air while in a sealed bell jar. Many studies since have shown little to no benefit of houseplants removing pollutants from the air in a home environment. This is in part because our houses are not airtight, and even if they were we would need hundreds, if not thousands, of plants in one room to make any difference to the air quality. While it is true that plants absorb carbon dioxide and emit oxygen during photosynthesis (see page 26), the levels of oxygen in the air would remain stable whether we had houseplants or not.

Myth: Bottom watering is best

There's a constant debate around whether it is better to water from the top or the bottom of a pot (see page 77). When watering from the bottom it is in fact the substrate that absorbs most of the water through capillary action, not the roots.

I prefer to water from the top of the pot, as you are less likely to oversaturate the substrate this way and have more control over the application.

Myth: Overwatering kills plants

This leads us onto the next popular myth. Giving too much water is often claimed to be the number one plant killer, but this usually isn't the only reason for a plant's demise (see page 83). The real problem is likely to be that the plant is not getting optimal light. Ensuring the correct light levels indoors allows your plant to photosynthesize more effectively and use all the water you give them. Be aware, too, that different substrates will require different amounts of water, as some retain moisture better than others. So always tailor your watering accordingly, taking this into account.

Myth: Stick to a watering schedule

There are so many apps and diaries designed to give you a watering schedule and most care labels will tell you how often to water a specific plant. While these all act as a good reminder to check your plant, watering on a schedule doesn't work because plants don't grow on a schedule. Their growth is dependent on many factors, so watering once a week could be way too much for one plant and way too little for the same plant in a different home in differing conditions. I always recommend checking plants on the same day and at the same time each week. Routine is great, but get to know your plants and provide care when they need it, not when a calendar dictates it.

Myth: Don't give plants tap water

Most days I will get asked what type of water I use for my plants, and people look surprised when I say tap water. Their response is usually 'doesn't the chlorine damage them?' It doesn't, mostly because plants can tolerate much higher levels of chlorine than the 5 PPM (parts per million) set out by the World Health Organization for drinking water, and in fact plants need a little chlorine, as it is essential for the chemical reaction that allows stomata to function effectively.

Myth: Homemade fertilizer is best

Every day I see a new recipe or 'hack' for a homemade miracle fertilizer. The videos and posts often show a plant's miraculous growth after being fed with a whole range of things from banana skins to eggshells. These fertilizers will never achieve such lush results, and they could cause problems for plants. This is because the natural materials used to make these fertilizers do not contain high levels of nutrients, nor the right ones for your plants. Even if the correct nutrients were provided, organic material such as banana skins and eggshells need to be broken down by microbes to make these nutrients available to your plants. Blending, steeping, or making teas from these ingredients doesn't do this either – you are giving your plants raw organic matter that feeds fungus, which attracts fungus gnats (see page 158). This nutrient soup also encourages potentially harmful pathogenic bacteria, which can lead to root rot (see page 83). Far better to add waste ingredients to a compost heap, let nature do its work, and use the resulting mix on outdoor plants. Your indoor plants will thank you for investing in some tailored houseplant fertilizer instead.

Myth: Stop fertilizing in winter

Houseplants don't recognize winter while in our homes, and most tropical plants in their natural environments have a wet and dry season or just a single climate all year, so 'winter' isn't really in their DNA. Most homes remain above 10–15°C (50–59°F) during winter, and if your plants receive enough light they will continue to grow. If your plant is growing, provide it with the nutrients to do so most effectively, whatever the weather outside. There's no one rule fits all, so just get to know your plants' growth and increase or decrease fertilizing in line with how much you are watering. This usually reflects the speed of their growth – plants use more water when growing faster and less if they slow down. This is why as a general rule I recommend using fertilizer with every other watering (see page 108).

Myth: A little polish makes leaves shine

There are myriad options from home remedies such as banana skins, milk, mayonnaise, and various cooking oils, to a range of products manufactured for the purpose. What they all have in common is that they are not required, and may also damage your plants and impede their growth.

Anything oily applied to leaves will clog the stomata and slow gas exchange during photosynthesis (see page 26). An artificially shined leaf will also reflect more light away, and when most plants don't receive enough light in our homes this isn't helpful (see page 29). The coating left on leaves traps more dust and dirt and interferes with a plant's natural defences against pests and disease. If you really want to clean leaves, wipe them with a damp cloth (see page 29).

Myth: Misting increases humidity

It's often claimed that misting plants will increase the relative humidity in the direct environment around them, but unless the plants are growing in an enclosed area such as a terrarium or greenhouse (see page 89), this is not the case. This is because the water evaporates so quickly, with the vapour dispersing into the surrounding air pretty much immediately, leaving the humidity almost exactly as it was before within minutes. In fact, misting can be detrimental, because plants like stability and these fluctuations in humidity don't help it to regulate its processes. In addition, any water left unevaporated on the leaves creates the perfect atmosphere for fungus to grow. Many people love misting and find it relaxing, which I get, so if you are a mister, try to do it at the beginning of the day and create some extra space and airflow around the plants to help the leaves to dry out and thus avoid any problems.

Myth: I can't grow plants

Many people tell me how beautiful the plants in the shop are, then say they can't keep any because they are a 'plant killer'. I see this as my mission to disprove their theory. Usually people feel this way because they have bought the wrong plant for their home environment, or maybe they didn't have the right care knowledge. Although I do believe some people are more in tune with nature than others, plant care can be learned easily. With some guidance and the acceptance that you will inevitably lose a few plants along the way as part of the learning experience, anyone can develop the knack for growing successfully.

Glossary

Abiotic disease
Non-infectious disease, often caused by factors such as nutrient deficiency or poor air quality.

Anthocyanins
A group of deep red, purple, and blue pigments found in plants.

Aroid
The common name for members of the *Araceae* family of plants, or the Philodendron or Arum family.

Arthropods
Invertebrate animals with an exoskeleton, segmented body, and paired jointed limbs. Divided into four groups: insects, myriapods, arachnids, crustaceans.

Autotroph
An organism that can produce its own food using light, water, and carbon dioxide, or other chemicals.

Axillary bud/axils
The bud of a shoot located in the axil of a leaf (the angle between the leaf or stem and the leaf or branch that supports it).

Beneficial microbes
Microorganisms that are beneficial to plant health by making nutrients available to plants, or as biocontrol in preventing pests, parasites, or diseases, such as mycorrhizal fungi or nitrogen-fixing bacteria.

Bio-active
A compound that has an effect on a living organism, tissue, or cell.

Bract
A modified or specialized leaf that grows just below a flower – it is sometimes mistaken for a flower.

CAM (crassulacean acid metabolism)
A specialized method of photosynthesis that allows a plant to take in carbon dioxide overnight through stomata that open at night instead of during the day in order to reduce water loss through evaporation.

Capillary action
This is the movement of water through a plant from the roots without the support of and often in opposition to gravity.

Chlorophyll
Green chlorophyll is located within the chloroplasts of a plant cell and absorbs the light energy needed for photosynthesis.

Chloroplasts
These organelles are located in the plant cells and contain the green pigment chlorophyll.

CITES appendix
Three appendices listing species according to the level of protection they need. From Appendix I – those threatened with extinction, up to Appendix III – the trade of which is controlled.

Epiphyte
A plant that grows on tree branches or cliffs that derives nutrients from the air and rain.

Extrafloral nectaries
Nectar-secreting glands located away from the flower that attract pollinators but are not part of pollination, thus 'extrafloral'.

Family
A group of plants that are a related species and tend to share physical characteristics.

Fenestrations
From the Latin word for 'window', these are holes or openings in a plant leaf.

Foot candle (FC)
A measurement of light intensity that records the light level reaching the surface of the plant; knowing your light level in your home will allow you to choose a plant that will thrive and grow there.

Fungicide
A pesticide that kills or prevents the growth of fungi and their spores.

Genus
A group of plants that are more closely related than a family, and which share one or more characteristic.

Guttation
The appearance of little droplets of liquid on leaves as plants expel excess water and nutrients to balance levels within the plant.

Habit
Also referred to as form; the characteristic shape, appearance, or growth of a plant.

Habitat
Simply, the place where a plant lives, often these environments have specific characteristics, such as rainforest, woodland, or desert.

Harden off
The process of acclimatizing plants to cooler temperatures or lower humidity.

Hemiepiphyte
A plant that spends part of its life cycle as an epiphyte – they may grow on a host plant but later establish root contact with a substrate.

Hermaphrodite
These are plants that have male and female reproductive organs within the same flower.

Hybrid
A plant that results from the cross-pollination of two different plant varieties.

Hydrophobic
Something that repels and therefore does not absorb water.

Inflorescence
A group or cluster of flowers arranged on a stem that is composed of a main branch or arrangement of branches.

Light meter
A device that will tell you the brightness of your space, often giving the reading in foot candles, to determine if there is sufficient light for your plants.

Macronutrients
Nutrients that plants need in substantial quantities for optimal growth.

Micronutrients
Nutrients that plants need for growth, but in smaller quantities than macronutrients.

Morphology
The study of the size, shape, and structure of plants.

Mother plant
The plant from which cuttings are taken.

Mutation
A naturally occurring genetic mutation that can cause a change in the appearance of a plant – such as in form, foliage colour, flecks in a flower, etc.

Mycorrhizal fungi
Beneficial fungi that that grow around the root system of a plant and increase the water and nutrient abilities of the roots.

Nomenclature
The system for the naming of plants.

NPK
The three major nutrients required by a plant: Nitrogen (N), Phosphorus (P), and Potassium (K).

PCD, or programmed cell death
A genetically controlled process by which plants can get rid of damaged cells or those that are no longer needed.

Petiole
The stalk of a leaf.

Photosynthesis
The process by which plants use sunlight, water, and carbon dioxide to create oxygen and energy in the form of glucose (sugar).

Phototropism
The growth of a plant's stems towards the direction of the light source, which can cause a leaning or bent appearance.

Pollination
The process of transferring pollen grains from the male anther of a flower to the female stigma for fertilization and the production of a seed.

Propagation
The process of creating new plants; this can be either from seeds or leaf, stem, or root cuttings.

Propagator
An incubator for your seeds and young plants, which will provide warmth to get plants started in the early stages of growth.

Reversion
This is when a plant cultivar has a particular leaf colour, shape, or other stand-out characteristic that is lost when it reverts back to an earlier form of the plant's appearance.

Root stimulator
A product that contains the hormone (auxin), which encourages a stronger root system in young plants. It can be added to water and watered into the roots.

Spadix
A spike of minute flowers held on a fleshy stem of a plant, common in the Araceae family (e.g. Philodendron).

Spathe
A bract that wraps around an inflorescence, or a pair of bracts that together enclose the inflorescence, usually found around a spadix.

Stomata
Tiny holes located on the underside of leaves that open and close to control water loss and gas exchange in photosynthesis.

Substrate
The surface on which a plant lives – e.g. soil, rock, or moss.

Thermogenesis
The process of heat production to raise the temperature of a plant above that of the surrounding air – for example, in the Titan arum (*Amorphophallus titanum*), often in order to attract pollinating insects.

Thigmomorphogenesis
The response of a plant to touch or another sensation, such as wind.

Tissue culture
Process by which fragments of tissue from plants are grown in an artificial medium away from the parent plant to produce new plants.

Tuber
A thickened underground part of a stem of a plant, used by the plant as a storage organ for nutrients.

Variegation
The appearance of different markings or colours on leaves or stems of a plant.

Xylem vessels
Vascular tissue in a plant that transports water and minerals from the roots up through the stems and into the leaves.

Resources

Useful websites

powo.science.kew.org

worldfloraonline.org

rhs.org.uk

gbif.org

Podcasts

On The Ledge janeperrone.com

Plant Daddy plantdaddypodcast.com

In Defense of Plants indefenseofplants.com

Books

D. G. Hessayon, *The House Plant Expert Books* (Transworld, 1996)

Darryl Cheng, *The New Plant Parent* (Abrams Image, 2019)

Gardening accessories

Watering cans and misters haws.co.uk

Secateurs and snips niwaki.com

Peat-free compost dalefootcomposts.co.uk

Workshops and further learning

notanotherjungle.com
Instagram @notanotherjungle

Bibliography

Studies

B. C. Wolverton, Anne Johnson, and Keith Bounds; "**Interior Landscape Plants For Indoor Air Pollution Abatement**"; ntrs.nasa.gov/citations/19930073077 (15 September 1989)

Jianjun Chen, Dennis B. McConnell, and Richard J. Henny; "**Light-induced coordinative changes in leaf variegation between mother plants and daughter plantlets of chlorophytum comosum 'vittatum'**"; researchgate.net/ publication/283372700_Light_induced_ coordinative_changes_in_leaf_variegation_ between_mother_plants_and_daughter_ plantlets_of_chlorophytum_ comosum_%27vittatum%27 (November 2004)

Oren Shelef, Liron Summerfield, Simcha Lev-Yadun, Santiago Villamarin-Cortez, Roy Sadeh, Ittai Herrmann, and Shimon Rachmilevitch; "**Thermal Benefits From White Variegation of *Silybum marianum* Leaves; Frontiers in Plant Science**"; ncbi. nlm.nih.gov/pmc/articles/PMC6543541 (24 May 2019)

"**Department of Environment and Natural Resources IX warns plant poachers on illegal collection of wild plants**"; r9.denr.gov.ph/ index.php/news-events/press-releases/1337- denr-ix-warns-plant-poachers-on-illegal- collection-of-wild-plants (14 September 2020)

Min-sun Lee, Juyoung Lee, Bum-Jin Park, and Yoshifumi Miyazaki; "**Interaction with indoor plants may reduce psychological and physiological stress by suppressing autonomic nervous system activity in young adults**"; ncbi.nlm.nih.gov/pmc/articles/ PMC4419447/ (28 April 2015)

Charles Hall and Melinda Knuth; "**An Update of the Literature Supporting the Well-Being Benefits of Plants: A Review of the Emotional and Mental Health Benefits of Plants**"; cdn.americainbloom.org/ wp-content/uploads/2022/01/Well-Being- Benefits-of-Plants-Charlie-Hall-3.pdf

RHS; "**Houseplants: to support human health**"; rhs.org.uk/plants/types/houseplants/ for-human-health

Tina Bringslimark, Terry Hartig, and Grete Grindal Patil; "**Psychological Benefits of Indoor Plants in Workplaces: Putting Experimental Results into Context**"; journals.ashs.org/hortsci/view/journals/ hortsci/42/3/article-p581.xml (June 2007)

Ruohan Wang and Zhixiang Zhang; "**Floral thermogenesis: An adaptive strategy of pollination biology in Magnoliaceae**"; ncbi. nlm.nih.gov/pmc/articles/PMC4594551/ (9 March 2015)

Botanical websites

cactus-art.biz/schede/GEOHINTONIA/ Geohintonia_mexicana/Geohintonia_ mexicana/Geohintonia_mexicana.htm

janeperrone.com/on-the-ledge/thrips

Index

Page numbers in *italics* refer to illustrations

Acknowledgments

Author acknowledgments

Without the support and encouragement of my Grandad Dave and my late Nana Cora my interest in plants and the natural world would not have been cultivated into what it is today, so I must thank them first with endless gratitude.

The team at DK guided me through my first ever book and helped me create something I'm unbelievably proud of. A special thanks to Chris Young for his support throughout this whole process, Katie Cowan, Ruth O'Rourke, and Lucy Philpott, my amazing editor. Also thanks to the DK design team – Barbara Zuniga, Maxine Pedliham, and Marianne Markham; seeing the book evolve into what it has become has been very special.

Helena Caldon supported me in editing and proofreading my writing and was an absolute joy to work with. Most importantly, thank you for your understanding in the way I work. A special mention to designer Vicky Read for creating something truly beautiful.

Photographer Jason Ingram's incredible work perfectly captures the beauty and personality of my plants. The shoot days were real highlights of this whole process.

Thanks also to Jo Lightfoot for getting this project off the ground.

Outside of the book team I have a wonderful group of planty friends, botanists, and growers who have supported and inspired me throughout the process and on my horticultural journey. Thank you to each and every one of you, and a special thank you to Mo (@thebotanicalarchive) and Martin (@bigcactusrescue) for trusting me with some of your plants for the photoshoot, and to Rogier (@Rogiervanvugt) for the image of the Amorphophallus in bloom and the information on its flowering.

Publisher acknowledgments

DK would like to thank Kathy Steer for proofreading, Vanessa Bird for indexing, Adam Brackenbury for repro work, and Giulia Garden for the original design concept. Thanks also goes to Martin @bigcactusrescue for providing the cacti photographed on pages 114 and 115 and Mo @thebotanicalarchive for providing the *Philodendron spiritus-sancti* photographed on page 136.

Picture credits

The publisher would like to thank the following for their kind permission to reproduce their photographs:

(Key: a-above; b-below/bottom; c-centre; f-far; l-left; r-right; t-top)

Dreamstime.com: Iakov Filimonov 172; **Getty Images / iStock:** DigitalVision Vectors / Grafissimo 169; **Tony Le-Britton:** 34, 52tr, 52br, 53, 151, 173, 174–175; **Rogier van Vugt:** 131

All other images © Dorling Kindersley

DK | Penguin Random House

Editor Lucy Philpott
Senior Designer Barbara Zuniga
Senior Production Editor Tony Phipps
Senior Production Controller Samantha Cross
Jackets Coordinator Jasmin Lennie
Editorial Manager Ruth O'Rourke
Design Manager Marianne Markham
Art Director Maxine Pedliham
Publishing Director Katie Cowan

Editor Helena Caldon
Designer Vicky Read
Photographer Jason Ingram
Illustrator SJC Illustration
Consultant Gardening Publisher Chris Young

First published in Great Britain in 2023 by
Dorling Kindersley Limited, DK, One Embassy Gardens, 8 Viaduct Gardens,
London, SW11 7BW

The authorised representative in the EEA is
Dorling Kindersley Verlag GmbH. Arnulfstr. 124, 80636 Munich, Germany

Text copyright © Tony Le-Britton 2023

A CIP catalogue record for this book
is available from the British Library.
ISBN: 978-0-2415-7235-1

Printed and bound in China

For the curious
www.dk.com

MIX
Paper | Supporting
responsible forestry
FSC™ C018179

This book was made with Forest
Stewardship Council™ certified paper—
one small step in DK's commitment to
a sustainable future. For more information
go to www.dk.com/our-green-pledge

About the author

Tony Le-Britton is a self-taught houseplant grower and prolific collector of some of the world's rarest plants. Growing up in Newcastle, Tony was taught to garden as a child by his grandparents; his debut book is the culmination of 30 years of growing experience and plant knowledge. In 2020, he set up his Instagram account @notanotherjungle to share his passion for plants, advice on plant care, and stunning photography, and since then it has built up over 170,000 followers. Now living in Northamptonshire with his two dogs, Fig and Bow, in 2022 Tony opened his first shop, selling a plethora of popular and more unusual houseplants. National press features include *Sunday Times*, *Mirror*, and *Metro*, as well as radio and TV appearances, notably BBC *Gardeners' World*. Tony is also one of the most celebrated hair and beauty photographers in the UK.